GOPRO®:

HOW TO USE THE GOPRO®

HERO 7

SILVER & WHITE

PUBLISHED BY **Kaisanti Press**

GOPRO: HOW TO USE THE GOPRO HERO 7 SILVER AND WHITE.

FIRST EDITION: October 2018

Copyright

Trademarks

This book is in no way affiliated, authorized, sponsored, or endorsed by GoPro, Inc. or any other companies mentioned in this book. All references to GoPro and other trademarked properties are used in accordance with the Nominative Fair Use Doctrine and are not meant to imply that this book is a GoPro, Inc. product for advertising or other commercial purposes.

All terms mentioned in this book that are known to be trademarks or service marks have been appropriately capitalized. The author cannot attest to the accuracy of this information. Use of a term in the book should not be regarded as affecting the validity of any trademark or service mark.

GoPro®, HERO®, SuperView® & 3-Way® are trademarks or registered trademarks of GoPro, Inc. in the United States and other countries. Any other trademarks remain property of the trademark holder.

Warning and Disclaimer

This book nor its author does not endorse any of the dangerous sports/activities shown in this book. If you choose to participate in these activities, do so at your own risk. This book does not guarantee that by following the advice in this book, your camera will not be damaged. Always refer to your camera's user manual. Always check with your camera manufacturer and follow recommendations before getting your camera wet. The author accepts no liability for any harm done to your camera or selves.

GOPRO®:

HOW TO USE THE GOPRO®

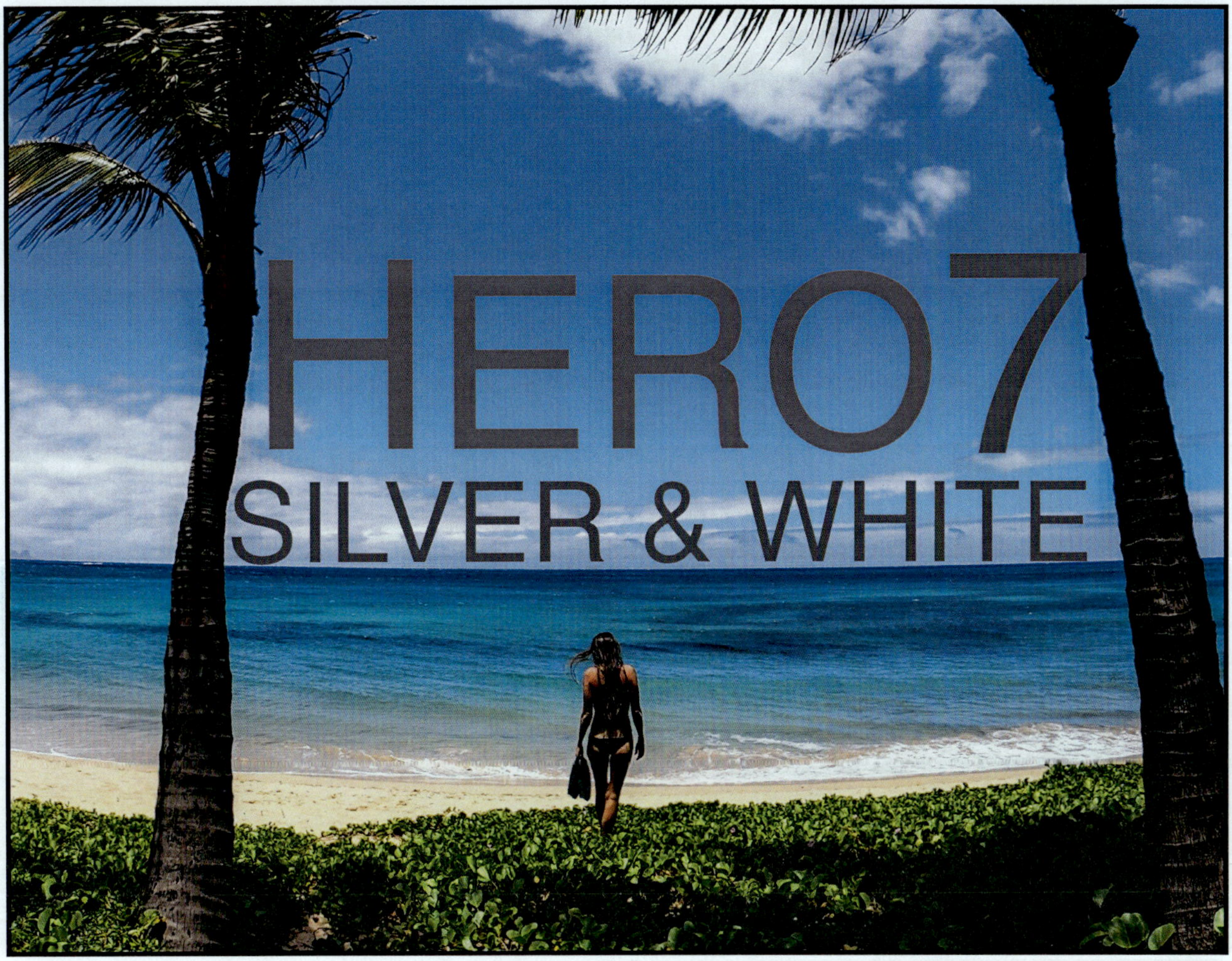

HERO7 SILVER & WHITE

The Essential Book for The Hero 7 Silver & White

by Jordan Hetrick

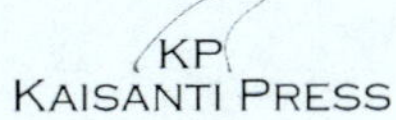

“Taking an image, freezing a moment,

reveals how rich reality truly is.”

~Anonymous

INTRODUCTION

That little GoPro camera you hold in your hand is the result of years of testing, revising, and perfecting. What started as a simple desire to carry a camera for surfing pics of some friends grew, grew, and grew some more.

The same convenience that GoPro founder Nick Woodman was searching for when he strapped a camera onto his wrist is what has attracted millions of people to these powerful storytelling devices. Everyone has moments in his or her life to be remembered, and there is no easier way to record them than with a GoPro camera. These cameras are waterproof, shockproof, tough little cameras that are fully capable of recording life's moments in such crisp, clear high quality that we can replay them over and over to feel like we are there again.

When the first GoPro was released, I had already been using big, bulky water housings to take photos of surfers, bodyboarders and windsurfers around the world for years. The resulting images were worth the hard work, but when I got my first GoPro camera, the struggle of the big camera was gone and just the fun remained. That's when it all clicked. Everyone was going to want one of these, and people were going to need help. So I set out on a mission to figure out the clearest, most logical way for people to learn how to use their GoPro cameras from start to finish.

Eight years, twelve books, and millions of readers/viewers later, you are reading the evolution of my intent to help you, written specifically for the GoPro HERO7 Silver and White cameras.

This how-to-use guide will teach you how to use your HERO7 Silver or White camera with confidence from the initial setup all the way through to sharing your edited photos and videos. Let me teach you everything you need to know. I'm so happy to have you on board!

Jordan Hetrick

Bestselling Author on GoPro Cameras

CONTENTS

CONTENTS

The Camera Follows Behind The Subject

CONTENTS

WHERE WOULD YOU LIKE TO SHARE THIS?

GOPRO061.JPG

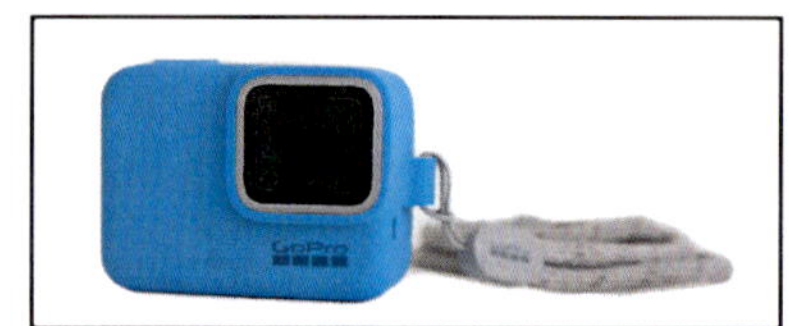

ABOUT THE HERO7 SILVER & WHITE

When it comes to easy filming on the go, the Hero7 Silver and White cameras are the essence of simplicity. In contrast to the Hero7 Black which has every bell and whistle available, the Silver and White cameras offer a simplified filming experience for the recreational user who just wants an easy, durable camera to capture life's best moments.

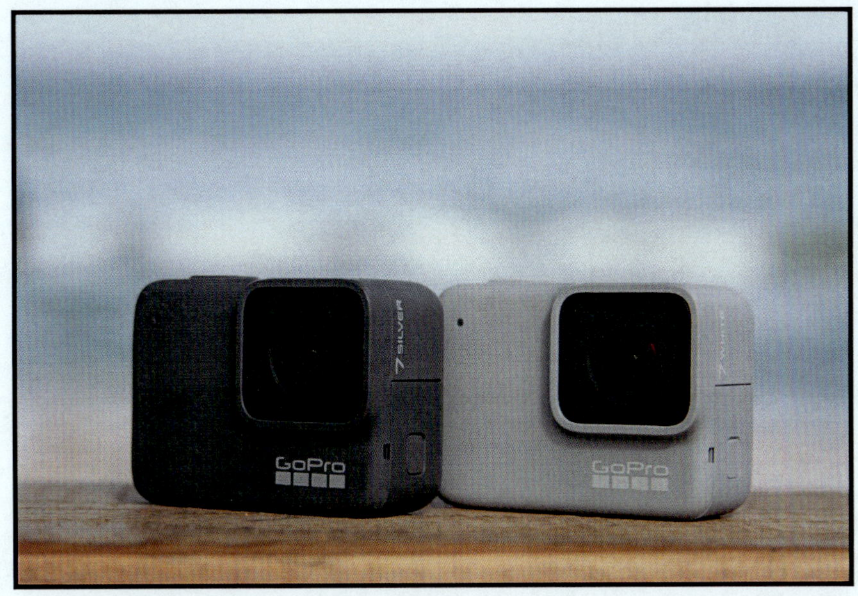

The Silver and White cameras are more alike than they are different. Both cameras are waterproof to 33' and have most of their components, such as the lens cover and battery, built in to the camera for simplicity. The front display screen seen on many of the other models is missing, but they both have rear Touch Screens for composing your shots and viewing media. The Touch Screen icons are virtually the same and many of the settings mimic each other.

Both cameras record 1440p video and the Silver also offers 4k video with the touch of an icon. There are also a few other differences we will cover as we make our way through the learning process.

Even though these camera models are designed to be simple, for those of you interested in improving your media and expanding your filming knowledge, your new camera is the perfect entry point into the GoPro world. So grab your Hero7 Silver or White and let's learn everything you need to know about your new camera to start recording memories you will want to watch forever!

HOW TO USE THIS GUIDE

Now that you've decided to really learn how to use your GoPro® HERO7 camera, the information in this guide will teach you everything you need to know to get the shots you've always wanted.

This guide is organized into 7 Steps, which were written to logically guide you through the learning process. By the end of this book, you will have a clear and thorough knowledge of your GoPro Hero7 camera and everything about the GoPro world.

In Step One- Get To Know Your HERO7, you will learn how to unlock the full potential of your new camera. This section includes essential information to familiarize you with your camera and to get you started, as well as get you connected to the GoPro App. You can also download the HERO7 Silver or White User Manual from GoPro's Support page on their website to be used in conjunction with the information in this guide. Your camera's User Manual tells you all of the little details about every setting option, while this guide provides you with the vital knowledge to understand what you really need to know to use your HERO7.

The Go Deeper sections provide more advanced tips for using your HERO7 camera. You may want to revisit these sections after learning the basics.

If you just bought your camera, before you buy the wrong mounts for your lifestyle, check out the Mounting Section in Step 3 to see which mounts are right for you and your passions!

Take your time, go step by step and by the time you finish this book, you will finally know how to use your HERO7 camera to record, edit and share life's most memorable moments!

STEP ONE

GET TO KNOW YOUR HERO7

Learn To Navigate Your New Camera

Welcome to the HERO7! This first section gives you hands on practice to easily navigate your new camera and access its features so you can focus on filming. Once you know your way around, you will be able to unlock the full potential of the HERO7 to capture your exciting moments in the best way possible.

So let's get to know your new camera!

SETTING UP YOUR CAMERA FOR THE FIRST TIME (It's Easy!)

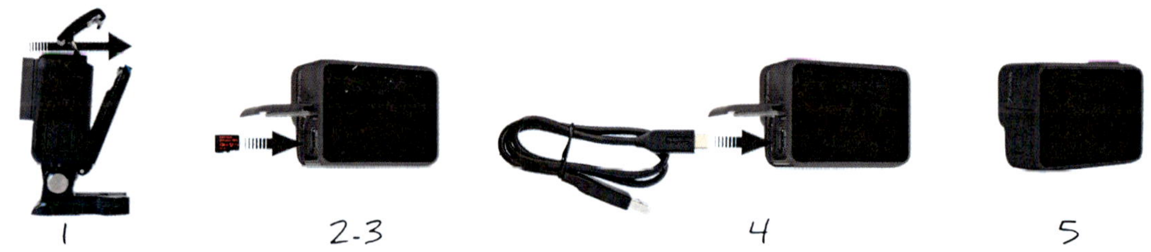

1. **Remove your camera from the frame** by lifting the latch on the Frame from the front of the camera. Lower the back door and slide the camera out.

2. Open the **side door on the right side** of your camera by pressing the Latch Release Button and sliding down.

3. **Insert the microSD Card** with the text facing the front of the camera. A 32GB microSD card is included in some HERO7 kits as a bonus. The Silver/White requires a Class 10 or UHS-1 microSD card up to 128GB (such as the SanDisk Extreme UHS-1), although some cards up to 256GB (such as the Samsung EVO Select) are compatible. Lexar, SanDisk and Samsung are the most well-known brands. See the microSD chart in the Troubleshooting section at the end of this book to make sure your card is recommended.

4. **Charge your camera.** Plug one end of the USB cable into the port on your camera and the other end to a computer or 5V/1-2A USB power supply. The built-in camera battery comes partially charged and using it with a partial charge will not affect the battery life. Charging typically takes about 2 hours.

5. The red light will turn off indicating that your camera has charged. Remove the USB cable and **close the side door**, making sure the door closes completely and the latch release button returns to its original position.

NOTE: The camera's firmware must be updated prior to the first use. The easiest way to update is to connect to the GoPro App on your phone or tablet, which you will learn how to do here in Step One. You can also update the firmware through Quik for Desktop on a computer. Make sure you are running the most current firmware (v01.50 or higher) to take advantage of the modes and settings as shown in this book. To see which version is installed on your camera, turn on your camera and swipe down from the top of the screen to expose the Dashboard and Preferences menu. The firmware version is located under Preferences>About>Camera Info

Your camera is ready to use. Now let's go through elements of your camera!

TIP: Hold onto the plate your camera was mounted on in the packaging. A lot of people throw this away, but it's like a free bonus mount that can come in handy. You can **drill holes through it**, **glue it to a surface**, or **cut it down to size** for a custom mount.

WHAT ARE THESE BUTTONS AND PORTS FOR?

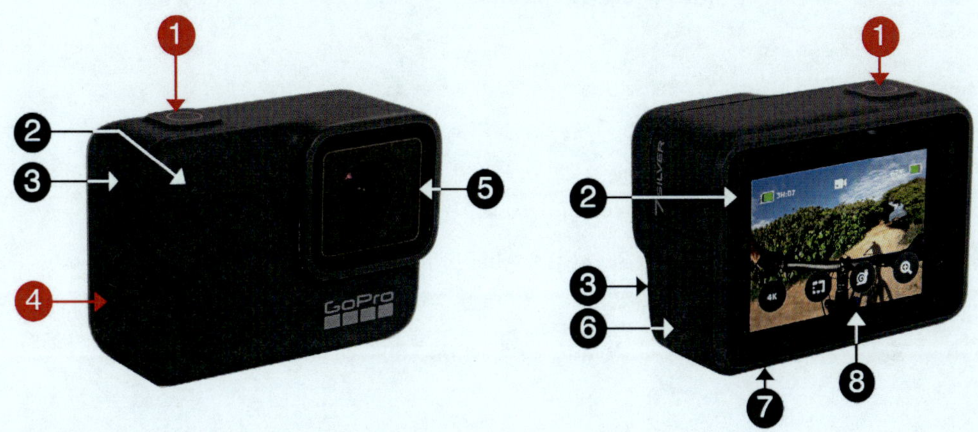

1. SHUTTER Button

Press this button to start and stop recording or to take photos.

2. Camera Status Lights

These red lights turn on when the camera is recording video and when taking photos. You can turn off the front light or all three of the lights (one is also on the bottom) in the Preferences Menu>General.

3. Microphones

The two microphones record audio.

4. POWER/MODE Button

Press this button to turn your camera ON.

Once your camera is powered on, press this button to scroll through shooting modes. Press this button to escape out of Settings or Media screens for a quick return to shooting modes.

Hold down this button down for 3 seconds to turn your camera OFF.

5. Lens Port

This glass element protects your camera's lens. The lens port is not replaceable on the HERO7 Silver or White.

6. Latch Release Tab/Side Door

The USB-C port and microSD card slot are inside this door. The USB port is for charging and transferring files. Step-by-step instructions for transferring your files are provided in Step 5- Creation.

Always close this door completely before you begin filming. The rubber gasket inside keeps water out of your camera.

7. Speaker (underneath)

This speaker plays audio when watching videos on the Touch Screen.

8. Touch Screen

The Touch Screen is a built-in LCD Screen that can be used as a viewfinder for composing shots, to change settings and to play back your footage. The Touch Screen section gives you an explanation of everything you can do using this screen.

NAVIGATING YOUR HERO7

Let's turn your camera on and learn to navigate your new camera so you can tap into all of the fun features of this powerful little camera.

GoPro has given you a few options for getting around the HERO7, but the simplest way is to use the camera's integrated Touch Screen on the back of the camera. All of the modes, settings and setup options are available through the Touch Screen.

With the simplified setting options on the HERO7 Silver and White cameras (which we will get into in the next step), you will be able to get around your camera with ease. First, let's take a closer look at navigating using the Touch Screen.

If you want to take a moment to practice getting around, follow the steps to take a short tour.

1. **Press the Power/Mode Button on the left side of your camera to turn your camera on.** It may take a few seconds for your camera to power on.

2. By default, the camera **powers on in Video Mode**, which is indicated by the Video camera icon at the top of the screen in the middle. The HERO7 has three main modes. The three modes from left to right are: Time Lapse, Video, and Photo. **Swipe Right** for Time Lapse Video Mode. **Swipe Left** for Photo Mode. Then **Swipe back to Video Mode**. The icon at the top of the screen indicates your current mode. The next chapter will help you understand the various modes.

3. **Now, at the bottom of the Touch Screen, there are several setting options for the selected mode.** The next chapter will help you understand the available settings for each mode.

4. To begin recording after selecting your settings, you would press the top Shutter Button.

It's that simple!

> **TIP: Using the Buttons to Change Modes and Settings.** When the Touch Screen is inaccessible, you can easily change modes by pressing the Mode Button on the left side of your camera to scroll through Video, Photo, and Time Lapse Video modes, in that order.

QUIKCAPTURE (ONE BUTTON CONTROL)

QuikCapture enables you to power on your camera straight into recording without any standby time. When recording is finished, the camera automatically turns back off.

To use this feature, called QuikCapture, you need to first enable the feature when your camera is turned on. Swipe down from the top of the screen and tap the "Jumping Rabbit" icon.

When your camera is turned off and you want to get straight into recording, utilize QuikCapture for quick access to video recording with the push of a button. **To begin recording video, Press the top Shutter Button and your camera will power on and begin recording. Once you press the Shutter Button again, your camera stops recording and turns off.**

QuikCapture is a great tool for specific filming situations to avoid wasting battery life on standby time or if you are experiencing overheating. Note that if you have used your camera in the previous 12 hours, there is a relatively quick 2-3 second startup time when using QuikCapture. Startup time is slightly longer if you haven't turned on the camera recently.

THE TOUCH SCREEN

The Touch Screen is a very convenient feature of the HERO7 and one that was missing from the first few generations of GoPro cameras. The Touch Screen gives you the ability to preview and compose your shots, as well as see a Live View of how setting changes affect your videos and photos. If you like to get muddy or sandy, consider using GoPro's Screen Protectors to keep your Touch Screen scratch-free.

You've already learned how to navigate the Touch Screen to change modes and basic settings, but the following section provides more information about other useful ways to tap into the convenience of the Touch Screen.

USING THE TOUCH SCREEN

The Touch Screen serves three primary functions: to change settings, as a viewfinder, and to view your recorded photos and videos:

TO SELECT AND CHANGE SETTINGS

As you learned previously, all modes and settings can be changed using the Touch Screen.

The Touch Screen tells you the following information about your camera settings, modes and status:

1. Touch Zoom

Drag the slider to use Touch Zoom which you will learn more about in Step 2- Settings.

2. Battery Life

This displays the exact percentage of remaining battery life.

3. Camera Mode

This icon indicates which recording mode you are currently using (Video, Photo, or Time Lapse Video)

4. Time/Storage/Files

In Video Mode, this displays the remaining number of minutes you can record on your memory card at the current video resolution. (This time will change when you change settings because different file sizes require different amounts of memory.)

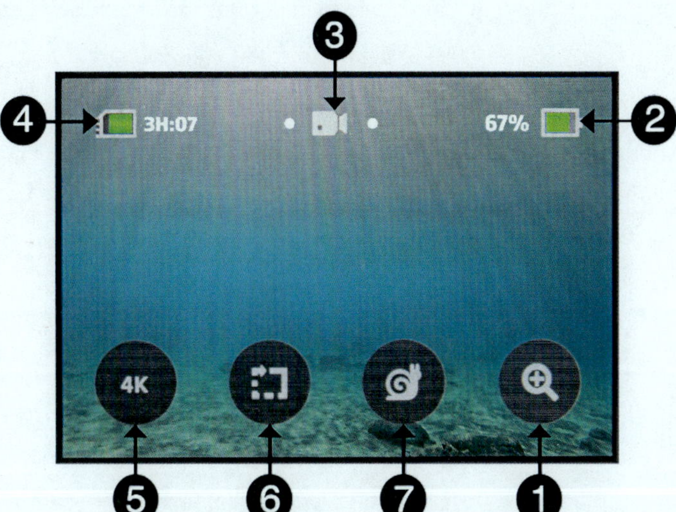

Video and Time Lapse Video Touch Display Screen

In Photo Modes, this tells you how many photos you have remaining at the current setting.

Video and Time Lapse Video Modes Only

5. 4k (Silver Only)

Tap this icon to record 4k Video. You will learn more about the benefits of 4k in Step 2- Settings.

6. Clip (Video Mode Only)

Record a 15 or 30 second video clip (depending on the setting you select in Preferences>Defaults>Clip Length).

7. Slow Motion (Video Mode Only)

Tap this icon to record videos that can be played back in slow motion. You will learn more about slow motion in Step 2- Settings.

Photo Mode Only

5. Burst

Tap this icon to take a speedy sequence of Burst photos. You will learn more about the using Burst Mode in Step 2- Settings.

6. Self-Timer

Set a self-timer for 3 seconds or 10 seconds.

• To show settings info (including current mode, the counter, capture settings and battery status) on the preview screen, **Tap the Screen**. To hide this info, Tap the Screen again. Hiding the info while you record allows you to see your shots more clearly for better composition.

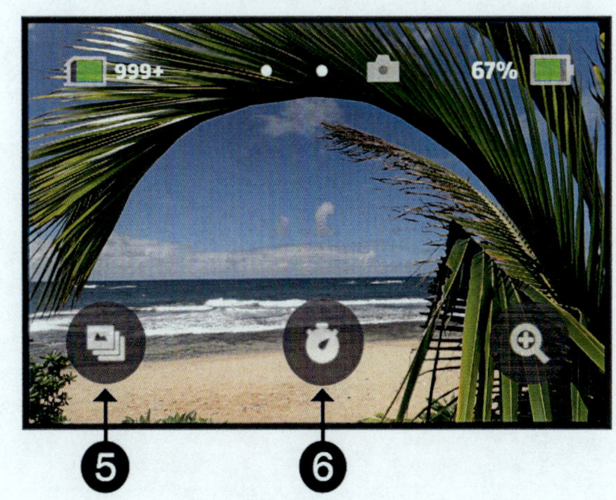

Photo Mode Touch Display Screen

AS A VIEWFINDER

The Touch Screen provides an easy way to **set up and compose your shots**. Use the Touch Screen to preview how your shots will look with the selected settings. After selecting your settings, Tap the Touch Screen to hide the icons for a clear screen.

When composing your shots through the Touch Screen as you film, keep the Touch Screen on when you want to watch the action. If the Touch Screen goes to sleep while you are filming, tap the screen or press the side Power/Mode Button to wake it back up. You may want to set the Screen Saver for a longer period (such as 3 minutes or Never) when recording long clips. You can set the Touch Screen to turn off after 1, 2, or 3 minutes (the time can be set in the Preferences Menu>Touch Screen>Screen Saver).

When using the Touch Screen **to set up mounted shots**, preview the composition on the Touch Screen. Once the shot is set up and your mounting position is secured, **let the Touch Screen go to sleep** to conserve battery life.

TO VIEW AND TRIM RECORDED PHOTOS AND VIDEOS

After a session, use the Touch Screen to view your videos and photos. One of the great things about your HERO7 is the instant gratification of seeing your photos and videos right away on the Touch Screen. The built-in screen lets you view your footage immediately.

The Touch Screen has some intelligent features, like recognizing if you recorded burst photos. Instead of scrolling through each photo of a Burst sequence, your camera batches them into one file for playback. The sequences are still available as separate photo files on your phone or computer.

- **Swipe Up** from the bottom of the screen to open your media. The diagram shows Touch Screen icons for playback. Icons will vary slightly depending on the type of media you are viewing.

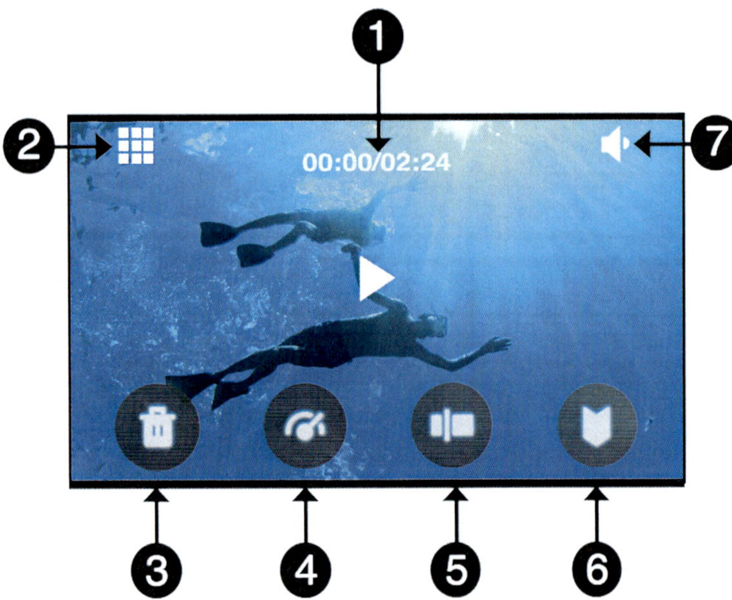

1. The **Time Counter** shows a running count of your play back time.
2. Select the **Grid Icon** to view thumbnails of your media.
3. Tap to **Delete** the current file.
4. Tap for **Slow Motion** playback. (Only displayed for videos recorded with the Slow Motion setting.)
5. **Scroll** through the timeline of a video clip.
6. Add a **Hilight** to your videos.
7. Raise or lower the **Audio** playback volume on your camera.

- **After tapping the Grid**, use the Gallery view to select files. To **Delete multiple files**, Tap the Check box in the top right corner, then the Trash Can icon to delete the selected files.
- **Scroll up** to view any photos or videos that you have already recorded. The most recent files are shown first.
- **Push play/pause in the middle of the screen** to watch the video, view a single shot photo or view a sequence of Burst photos.

VOICE CONTROL

At first, Voice Control seems a bit like a gimmick, but as you start to use it, you will realize that it's actually very useful, especially when using a GoPro. When your camera is out of reach, or your hands are busy, Voice Control gives you easy hands-free access to control your HERO7. With a simple command, you can start recording videos or taking photos. It's also much easier to change modes using Voice Control. Instead of swiping through the modes, you can go straight to the mode you want to record with.

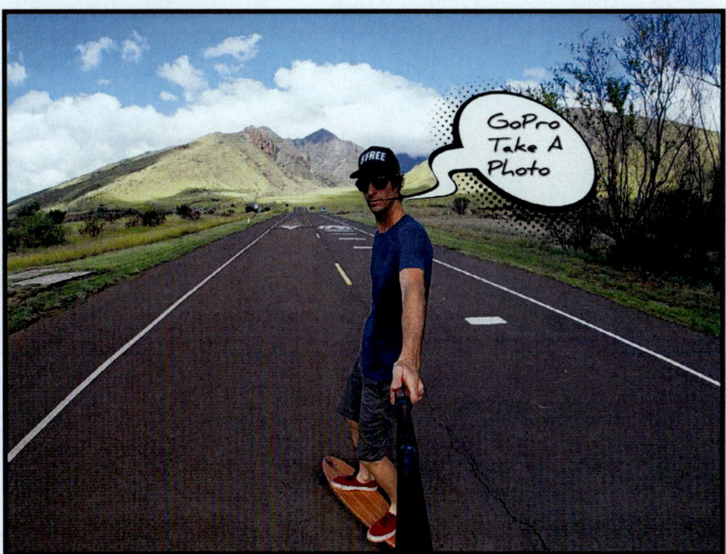

To activate Voice Control, Pull Down the top tray on the Touch Screen. Tap the Voice Control Icon at the middle left to remove the "x", turning the icon blue.

The preferred Voice Control language can be changed in the Preferences Menu (Preferences>Voice Control>Language).

You can't do everything with Voice Control, but there is a lot you can control. **Here is a list of the commands you can use with your HERO7:**

To Change Modes and Power Off

"GoPro Video Mode"
"GoPro Photo Mode"
"GoPro Time Lapse Mode"
"GoPro Burst Mode"
"GoPro Turn Off"

To Start and Stop Recording or Taking Photos

"GoPro Start Recording" (for video or time lapse, depending on current mode)
"GoPro Stop Recording" (for video or time lapse, depending on current mode)
"GoPro HiLight", "Oh Sh*t", "That was Sick" (all set a HiLight Tag)
"GoPro Take a Photo" (if your camera is not recording a video)
"GoPro Shoot Burst"
"GoPro Start Time Lapse"
"GoPro Stop Time Lapse"
"GoPro Capture" (captures photos or video in the current mode)
"GoPro Stop Capture"

Of course, as with anything, there are optimal times to use Voice Control and there are situations when Voice Control won't work too well. For best results, use Voice Control when there is **minimal ambient noise**. When recording video or a time lapse, you need to **stop recording** before issuing a new command.

Also, keep your GoPro **within a few feet** to make sure it can hear you, especially if there is ambient noise, such as the ocean or wind. Speak clearly and say the exact command.

Also, Voice Control will not work when your camera is underwater, or even sometimes after you have been in the water (if there is sand or water covering the mic opening). Make sure to shake your camera or blow any water out of the mic openings after going in the water.

WIFI / BLUETOOTH

The HERO7 uses a combination of 2.4 or 5GHz WiFi and Bluetooth to connect to a phone/tablet. Your camera emits its own signal, so you don't need to be within range of any WiFi signals to use your camera's WiFi features. Unlike older GoPro models, there is no indicator light or icon to tell you if your WiFi signal is on.

To access the Connections dialog, pull the top tray down on the Touch Screen. In Preferences, Tap Connections to access the WiFi settings. You can manually turn on or off the WiFi and connect to the GoPro App.

The HERO7 automatically manages your camera's WiFi, switching from WiFi to Bluetooth to reduce battery drain. If you will not be using your camera for an extended period, you may want to turn off the WiFi Signal. The drain on your battery is minimal, about 3% over 12 hours, but over time it could drain your battery if it hasn't turned off automatically.

USING THE GOPRO APP

The GoPro App works on your tablet or smartphone and is available for free from the App Store (iOS) or Google Play (Android).

In addition to giving you remote access to your camera's Shutter Button, modes and settings, the GoPro App allows you to view the action as you record videos and photos when you can't see your camera's Touch Screen. This is extremely useful for composing your mounted shots. You will see the benefit of this technology when you learn to set up your shots in Step 3-Mounting.

The GoPro App is also the easiest way to transfer photos and videos from your GoPro to your phone or tablet for sharing with friends and family.

TIP: Live View (viewing what you are filming while your camera is recording) compatibility depends on your device, but if you see a "Preview Not Available" message once you start recording, you are filming in a resolution that is not compatible with your device. Your camera is still able to record video, but you are not able to preview it using the App. If 4k is not working with your device, start with the Slow Motion setting to see if your device is compatible.

You can also **update your camera's firmware wirelessly through the App**. Updating your camera ensures that your camera is equipped with the most up-to-date features and settings. The App will notify you when an update is available.

TO CONNECT YOUR HERO7 TO THE GOPRO APP:

Download the GoPro App from your app store. The GoPro App is free so make sure you don't accidentally download an app that looks similar but charges a fee. There are no additional upgrade options for the GoPro App.

After you install and open the App, tap the camera icon in the top left corner. Then tap "Add a Camera". The App will walk you through the setup. When reconnecting to the App, make sure your camera's WiFi is turned on and the App will automatically prompt you to connect to your camera. If the WiFi Icon next to the image of your camera in the GoPro App is not blue (active), turn your camera on and the WiFi light will turn blue, allowing you to connect.

UNDERSTANDING THE APP

Once your camera is connected wirelessly to the App, the following buttons give you remote access to the full range of settings and modes on your HERO7:

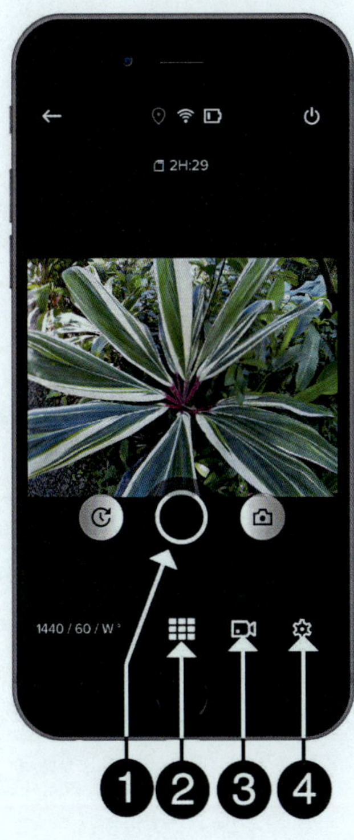

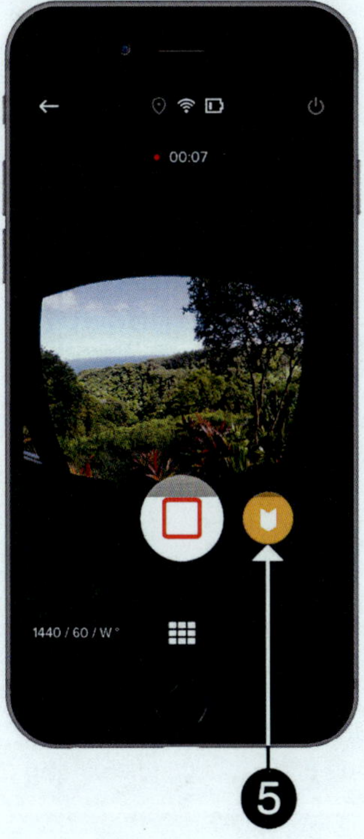

1. MODE/SHUTTER BUTTON

Swipe left or right to change between modes. Press the Circle Button on your selected mode to begin recording video or taking photos.

2. GOPRO MEDIA

Tap this icon to view the videos and photos that are currently on your camera's memory card. You can view, trim, download, delete and share these files.

3. MODE

This icon displays the current Mode since the main Icon becomes a Circle "Shutter" Button. You can also Tap this icon to select a different mode.

4. SETTINGS

This icon takes you to the Settings dialog, where you can change video and photo settings as well as access the Set Up Menu. In Step 2- Settings, you will learn which settings to use.

5. HILIGHT TAG (displayed only when recording video)

Press this button while recording video to add a HiLight Tag.

After filming, you can view, browse, delete, download and trim the content from your camera's memory card. If you plan on using GoPro's other mobile editing apps, you will need to save the photos and videos you want to use to your phone. If your phone is not compatible with the video resolution, when you download footage to your phone, the GoPro App automatically downsizes the footage for compatibility.

Quik STORIES The GoPro App can also automatically transfer the most recent files from your camera to your device to create an auto edit for you. This feature, called QuikStories, uses the GoPro App and Quik to make it easier than ever to share your most recent adventures. Learn more about using Quik and QuikStories in Step 5- Editing.

When you finish using the App, turn off your camera by pressing the power icon on the top right corner of the App screen. You can also turn your camera back on using the App if the camera's WiFi is still enabled.

Now that you've got your camera up and running, let's go to Step 2 to learn about the modes and settings.

STEP TWO

THE SETTINGS

Choose Your Settings to Get the Shot

When it comes to capturing unforgettable moments with your GoPro® HERO7, the options are endless. One of the biggest factors to recording those moments is setting up your shots correctly. Your HERO7 is a powerful little camera, capable of recording broadcast-quality video and eye-grabbing photos. But because these are GoPro's entry-level cameras, they simplified the modes and settings to make it easier for a first timer. To a new GoPro user, the options may be a bit hard to filter through. In this step, we will break it down and give you the simplified guide to your GoPro's settings and modes so you can learn which modes and settings to use and when.

Choosing the right settings with your finished product (video or photos) in mind is almost as important as the action you are recording. With the HERO7's simplified settings menus, once you get a basic understanding of the main recording modes, the rest will fall into place.

This step is separated into four sections to give you a rundown of which settings to choose whether you are shooting videos, photos, or time lapses. The fourth section highlights some of the useful general camera settings available in the Preferences menu to customize your filming experience. So, let's get into the business of having fun.

NOTE: Make sure your camera is running firmware version 01.50 or higher to be sure the following information matches your camera's settings.

RECORDING VIDEOS

Let's talk about recording videos with your HERO7. This section helps you understand how to use and choose the HERO7's video settings when recording videos with your HERO7 Silver or White.

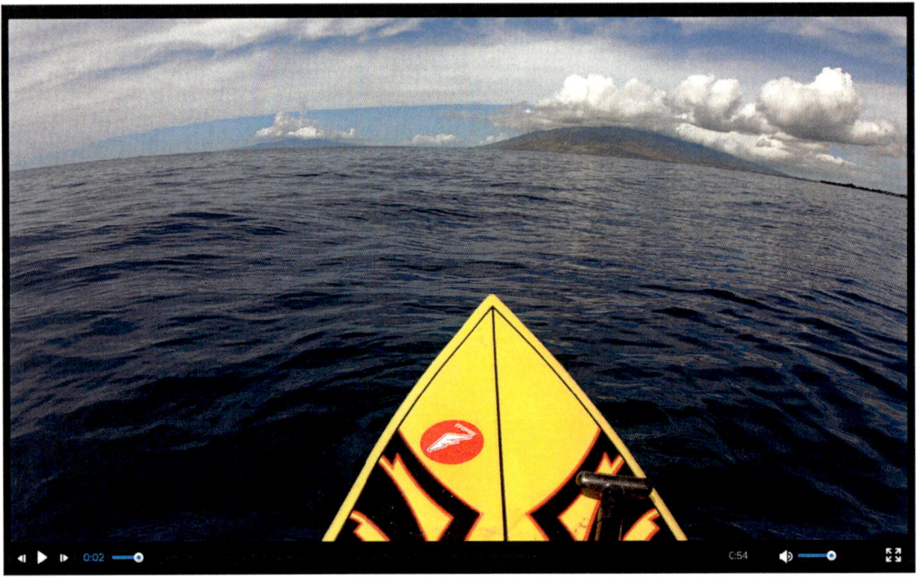

Video recorded on the HERO7 SILVER at 4k @ 30 FPS handheld.

VIDEO MODE

In Video Mode, your camera will **just record video**. Press the Shutter Button once to start recording video. Press the Shutter Button again to stop recording the clip. This is the mode to use to record video, whether you plan to play it back in regular speed or slow motion.

To record videos using Voice Control, say "GoPro Video Mode" to enter Mode. Then say "GoPro Start Recording" to record videos in video mode.

Choosing your VIDEO SETTINGS

Selecting the best video settings for your moment will help you achieve the shot you want and give you the freedom to edit your video how your mind envisions. Whether your camera is mounted near or far, you are filming fast action or scenery, full sun or low light, the settings you choose will give you the high quality footage you need when you begin editing your videos. There are only a few video settings available on the Hero7 Silver and White, so let's cover a few video basics before going over the best settings for your camera. Understanding the meaning of these simplified settings will help you dive below the surface and understand some key elements that will take your videos to the next level. If you decide to step up to one of the GoPro Black model cameras in the future, this deeper understanding will prepare you for the wide range of settings on the more advanced cameras.

There are three factors you should understand when choosing your video settings on the HERO7 and we will walk you through each one:

A) Understand what **File Size** and **Frame Rate** means

B) Learn how the **Aspect Ratio** affects your shot

C) **Select a setting** based on the type of action you are filming

A) UNDERSTAND WHAT FILE SIZE MEANS

The video settings are presented in a very simplified manner on the Hero7 Silver and White cameras, but behind the simple icons, there are a few terms that are important to understand when it comes to choosing your video settings. Video settings are defined in terms of resolution and frame rate, which is written like this- 1440p @ 30FPS or like this- 1440-30.

What does this mean? This refers to two things:

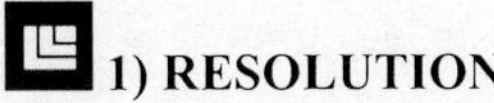

1) RESOLUTION

Resolution refers to the size of your video image. The first number before the dash ("1440" in 1440-30) tells you the size of the video image. So, why does resolution matter?

In simple terms, a video "image" is made up of a bunch of small dots, called pixels. A video comprised of many pixels creates a larger, more detailed image.

The resolution name (4k, 1440p, 1080p, etc.) defines how many lines of pixels exist within the video frame. The higher the number, the better the quality. The maximum resolution available on the HERO7 SILVER is 4k. As you can see in the chart below, a 4k video is much larger than a 1440p or 1080p video and produces more detailed video. The HERO7 White maxes out at 1440p

In 4k and 2.7k, the names refer to the width of the image in pixels. For example, a 4k video is about 4000 pixels wide (actually 3840px).

In 1440p, the number 1440 refers to the vertical height of the image being recorded. In other words, the image is 1,440 pixels high. (The "p" after the number stands for "progressive scan", which, without getting too technical, creates smoother, more detailed video).

This chart shows the relative pixel dimensions (width x height) of file sizes available on the HERO7 Silver and White (4k is not available on the White). 1080p is shown because 1440p can be cropped to 1080p for Widescreen playback.

On the HERO7 SILVER, you will use the Touch Screen icons to choose either 4k or 1440p.

The HERO7 WHITE records at 1440p only.

FPS 2) FRAMES PER SECOND (FPS)

The number after the dash (30 in this example) tells you how many frames are being recorded each second. **Frames Per Second (FPS)** refers to the number of individual frames (similar to photos) the camera records each second.

Capturing footage at a **higher frame rate (60 FPS) is better if you are planning to play back your footage in slow-mo**, which a lot of action clips need to look good. All of the video frame rates play back at regular speed by default. Slow motion is created when you change the rate at which the frames of a video are viewed. For example, if you record a 1 second clip at 60 frames per second, and you play it back at only 30 frames per second, it will take you 2 seconds to watch that 1 second clip. This effectively makes your video show in slow motion.

Recording more frames per second (60 FPS when the Slow Motion icon is blue) gives you the ability to slow down the footage from a high frame rate to a slower frame rate, such as 30 FPS, and still maintain that smooth film look.

What frame rate is acceptable?
Some film and video makers display their footage at 24 FPS because the on-screen "look" most closely matches film. Other professional video producers use 30 FPS as a standard frame rate, arguing that 24 FPS is only useful if you are transferring digital footage to film, which never really happens. 30 frames per second is better suited for viewing on televisions and computers. For simplicity, since the only two frame rates available with the HERO7 Silver and White are 30 FPS or 60 FPS, this book uses 30 frames per second as a standard.

If you want your footage to play in "slower" slow motion, you can conform your video to 24 frames per second and still maintain smooth video.

B) UNDERSTANDING ASPECT RATIO - 16:9 WIDESCREEN OR 4:3 STANDARD

WHAT IS AN ASPECT RATIO?

The Aspect Ratio (16:9 or 4:3) refers to the ratio (width: height) of the image you will capture. There are **two aspect ratios available on the Hero7 Silver. The Hero7 White only offers Standard 4:3.** However, you will want to edit many of your videos recorded from either camera to Widescreen, so read on to learn more about how the Aspect Ratio affects your composition:

16:9 WIDESCREEN ASPECT RATIO (4K)

• **16:9 Widescreen** is a widescreen format for HDTV's, plasma widescreen TV's, and cinema screens. This is how you see most videos and movies. YouTube, Vimeo and Hulu support this ratio. Using this ratio gives your footage the cool **widescreen cinematic look**. Widescreen is the **best choice for most shots when you have enough distance to capture what you want in the frame and you don't need slow motion**. 4k is the only 16:9 Widescreen resolution on the Hero7 Silver camera. 1080p is also a common Widescreen resolution you will use when editing your videos.

4:3 STANDARD ASPECT RATIO (1440P)

• **4:3 Standard** was the "default" ratio all videos used to be before widescreen came around. YouTube, Vimeo and Hulu also support this ratio, but you will see black bars on the sides so that the video fits in the widescreen player. The benefit of using a 4:3 ratio is that you capture the full frame, giving you **more top-to-bottom viewing area**. This makes it **easier to get your entire body in the shot**, especially when you are shooting at a close angle or when your camera is mounted on your body or equipment. The 4:3 resolution **can be used for point of view (POV) shots when your camera is mounted close to you**.

The Hero7 Silver and White both record videos at 1440p resolution, which is a Standard 4:3 Aspect Ratio. The fact that the Hero7 Silver and White uses a Standard Aspect Ratio as its default video resolution is a bit unconventional, but you will learn how to conform it to Widescreen when you edit if you choose to.

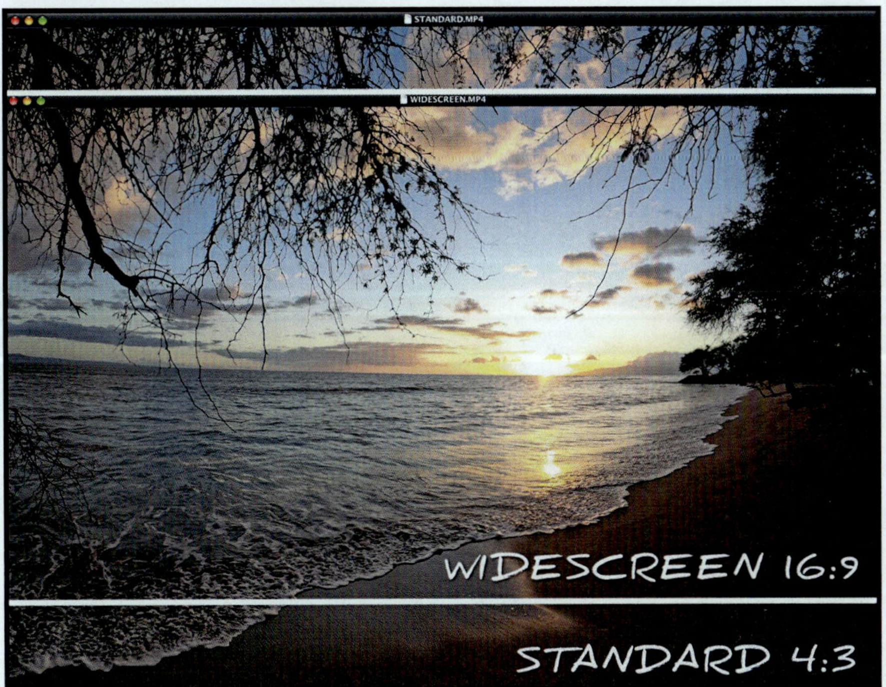

*The image above shows how the **Widescreen 16:9** shot in the middle crops out the top and bottom of what's captured in a **Standard 4:3** frame.*

TIP: When playing your videos online or on a computer, you will most often want to display your footage in a 16:9 Widescreen Aspect Ratio. Video footage filmed in a 4:3 Aspect Ratio will need to be edited to fit a widescreen frame. You can crop or scale 4:3 Aspect Ratio videos when editing to make them match Widescreen. (We will get to that in Step 5- Creation.) 1440p crops to 1080p without losing quality.

C) SELECT A SETTING BASED ON THE TYPE OF ACTION YOU ARE FILMING

You can select the right settings for your shot by using the icons on the touch screen. The following summary of the settings for the Hero7 Silver and White lets you know when to use each setting and why.

When choosing settings for a specific activity, consider the following tips:

TIP #1: Changing the frame rate for slow motion during editing will also affect the **audio speed**. Just because you record at a faster frame rate doesn't mean you must use the clip for slow motion. You can play a clip recorded at any frame rate in regular motion video. If you record a video clip at 30FPS and you want to play it at regular speed, when you export it to 24FPS, the extra 6 frames will be removed without affecting the audio.

TIP #2: PAL vs. NTSC: Most countries outside of North America use a format called PAL instead of NTSC. If you are in a country that uses PAL and your camera is set to shoot at PAL, the available frames per second rate will be different while using certain settings. The PAL frame rates that differ from the NTSC frame rates are noted below.

NTSC (in frames per second)	PAL (in frames per second)
30	25
60	50

THE HERO7 WHITE VIDEO SETTINGS

Check out this summary of the HERO7 WHITE's two video resolution options to help you find your favorites, depending on your scene.

1) "Slow Motion" 1440p @ 60 Frames Per Second

• This is your **go-to setting for the Hero7 White** and can be used almost all the time, **for both regular speed and slow motion** videos. There are only a few occasions when you may want to turn off Slow Motion- low light scenes and to use Touch Zoom.

• Tap the Slow Motion Icon on the Touch Screen to record in 1440-60 for slow motion or regular speed video.

• This resolution offers a **high frame rate of 60 frames per second**, which allows you to play back your footage at 2x slow motion (or 2.5x if you export at 24 frames per second). This resolution can also be played back at regular speed.

• 1440p can be edited to 1080p widescreen.

• If you are filming **in low light situations** (shady, cloudy, etc.), you may want to record at 30FPS because the higher frame rate is too fast for low light situations.

• Because 1440p is a Standard Aspect Ratio, it records more top to bottom area than a Widescreen shot. This aspect ratio **works well for mounted point of view shots** where the subject is close to the camera.

• Recommended scenes for this resolution include helmet-mounted shots, selfie polecam/handle shots, chest-mounted shots and most shots when you are wearing your camera.

2) "STANDARD VIDEO" (SLOW MOTION TURNED OFF) 1440P @ 30 FRAMES PER SECOND

• To use this resolution, make sure the Slow Motion icon is turned off.

• This is the **most basic video resolution available** on the Hero7 White and cannot be played back in slow motion because of the low frame rate.

• If you are filming in low light scenes, the slower frame rate of 30 FPS requires less light to make a high quality image and is a better choice than the 60 FPS resolution.

• The only time you really need to use this setting is **in low light situations** or if you want **to use Touch Zoom** to get closer to your subject.

THE HERO7 SILVER VIDEO SETTINGS

Check out this summary of the HERO7 SILVER's three video resolution options to help you find your favorites, depending on your scene.

1) "4K" WHICH IS REALLY 4K @ 30 FRAMES PER SECOND (4K-30)

• Tap the 4k Icon on the Touch Screen to record in 4k.

• 4k is a Widescreen 16:9 resolution.

• 4k is the **highest resolution available** on the Hero 7 Silver. 4k videos produce a video image of 3840px x 2160px. This image size can be viewed full size on YouTube and many computer screens. 4k video also gives you a lot of editing freedom when being edited to a 1080p video. Since 4k is 2x wider and taller than a 1080p video, you can zoom in up to 200% when editing and still maintain 1080p resolution.

• 30 frames per second is useful for videos played back at regular speed since the minimum frame rate for videos is 24 frames per second.

• If you are filming in **low light scenes**, the slower frame rate of 30 FPS requires less light to make a high quality image and is a better choice than the 60 FPS resolution.

• This setting is best used for **clips that do not require slow motion**, especially when you have your camera **mounted on a tripod or on a fixed object** with minimal shakiness. You can also choose this resolution when holding your camera as long as you keep your camera as steady as possible. (You will learn more filming tips in Step 4- Capture Your Action.)

• Whenever you don't need slow motion, 4k @ 30 FPS should be **your go-to setting for the highest quality, regular speed video** on the Hero7 Silver.

2) "SLOW MOTION" 1440P @ 60 FRAMES PER SECOND

• Tap the Slow Motion Icon on the Touch Screen to record in 1440-60 for slow motion.

• This resolution offers a higher frame rate of 60 frames per second, which allows you to play back your footage at 2x slow motion (or 2.5x if you export at 24 frames per second). This resolution can also be played back at regular speed.

• 1440p produces a much smaller video image than 4k which can be edited to 1080p widescreen.

• If you are filming in **low light situations** (shady, cloudy, etc.), you may want to record at **30FPS (4k) because the higher frame rate is too fast for low light situations**.

• Because 1440p is a Standard Aspect Ratio, it records more top to bottom area than a Widescreen shot (such as 4k). This aspect ratio works well for mounted point of view shots where the subject is close to the camera.

• **Recommended scenes** for this resolution include helmet-mounted shots, selfie polecam/handle shots, chest-mounted shots and most shots when you are wearing your camera.

• If you think you will want **to play back your video in slow motion, choose this setting**.

3) "STANDARD VIDEO" (4K AND SLOW MOTION TURNED OFF) 1440P @ 30 FRAMES PER SECOND

• To use this resolution, make sure the 4k and Slow Motion icons are turned off.

• This is the most basic video resolution combination available on the Hero7 Silver.

• The only time you really need to **use this setting is if you want to use Touch Zoom** to get closer to your subject.

OTHER USEFUL VIDEO SETTING OPTIONS

The following additional video settings give you even more control over the look and quality of your videos.

FOV TOUCH ZOOM

Touch Zoom gives you the freedom to fine-tune zoom to compose your shots exactly how you want them to look. Older GoPro cameras offered a Medium or Narrow FOV, but Touch Zoom gives you even more control over your composition. Use Touch Zoom to get closer to your subject or to film a more traditional 35mm-style shot.

Touch Zoom is adjusted by using the circle slider on the right side of the Touch Screen. Simply move the slider up to zoom in on your subject. Touch Zoom can be adjusted before or during recording. The HERO7 Silver and White cameras are the first GoPro cameras to feature the ability to Touch Zoom while recording a video, so take advantage of the new feature for some creative zoom shots!

The slider is grayed out in 4k and Slow Motion since these resolutions are not compatible with Touch Zoom. Touch Zoom can also be adjusted through the GoPro App directly on the Live Preview in compatible resolutions.

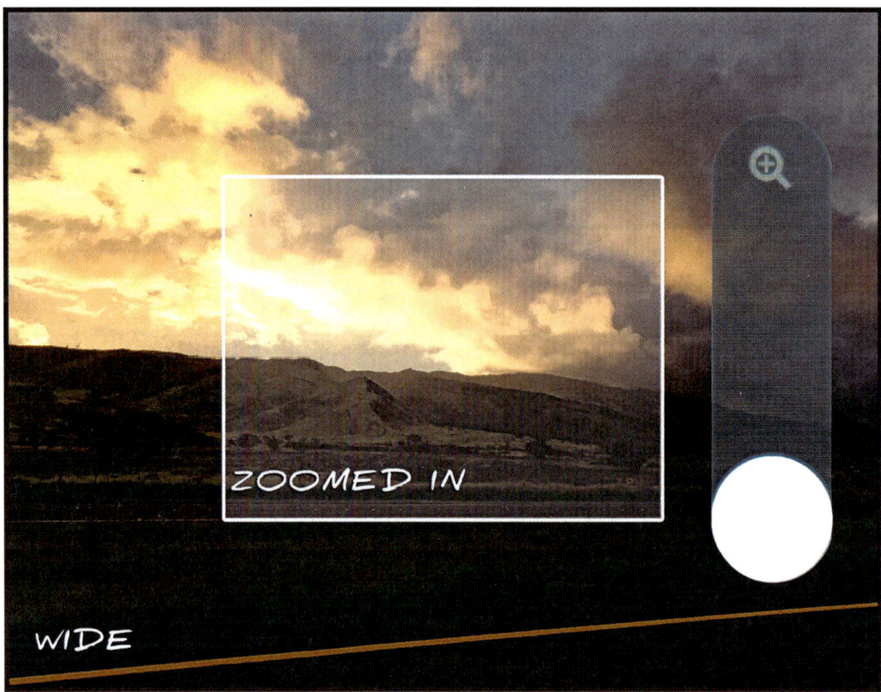

The white box represents the maximum zoom possible using Touch Zoom. When the zoom slider is all the way up, the image only includes the area in the white box creating tighter, less characteristically GoPro-looking shots.

Touch Zoom uses the extra size of the sensor when filming in 1440p to zoom in and maintain the selected resolution.

VIDEO STABILIZATION (EIS)

With the HERO7, all of your videos feature electronic image stabilization, which makes a huge difference in the overall look of your videos. The Standard Stabilization available on the HERO7 Silver and White is different from the HyperSmooth Stabilization on the HERO7 Black but still very effective to achieve smooth videos even for handheld shots.

Video stabilization keeps your footage steady, even when you are rocking and rolling, running or riding. An easy way to see the effects of stabilization is to hold your camera in a fixed direction and then move it side to side or up and down. The video movement will be much less noticeable than your actual movement.

Stabilization is automatically added to all of your videos, so you don't need to do anything. To create the stabilized videos, the camera's firmware uses the extra area outside of the frame to shift and rotate the video to keep your videos as smooth as possible.

Stabilization is more effective in shots that are zoomed in, so you can use Touch Zoom to achieve the best stabilization possible. However, you will most often need stabilization when your camera is mounted to you, so a zoomed in perspective is not quite as useful for body mounted shots.

Because your camera films stabilized shots but also needs the freedom to move-to pan, tilt, etc.- you can **give your camera's stabilization a helping hand by following these tips:**

• If you are filming in 1440p (without Slow Motion), **zoom in a little for better results**. When the field of view is zoomed in, the camera has more sensor to use for stabilization.

• Stabilization works **best when you have a specific focus or direction**. Stabilization is most effective for shots where a steady horizon would be natural, such as a chest-mounted mountain bike shot or driving offroad with the camera mounted to a vehicle. When you point in a more or less fixed direction, the camera's firmware knows which areas should be stabilized.

• Even though stabilization can smooth out shaky shots, **try to hold your camera steady and use smooth movements** when possible. When your camera is mounted on a pole or handle for handheld shots, hold your camera **upside down for stability**. The weight of the camera creates its own stability to steady the shots, especially for really shaky activities, such as running.

• Stabilization cannot compensate for a tilted horizon. When filming handheld shots where you have control of your camera, **keep an eye on the horizon and try to keep it as level as possible**. A crooked horizon, especially for cinematic style shots, should be avoided when possible.

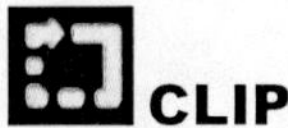 CLIP

When creating videos for sharing on mobile devices, the Clip feature gives you the power to automatically create 15 or 30 second clips. When you select one of these designated times, the video automatically stops recording after the set time. You can see the progression of the video indicated by a red line that goes around the screen. This red timeline can be used to plan out your short clips to get the content you want at just the right time.

To record a "Clip", tap the "15" or "30" icon on the bottom of the screen. Press the Shutter Button to record your clip and the clip will automatically stop recording after the selected time. You can stop recording a Clip early by pressing the Shutter Button again. The default clip time can be set to 15 or 30 seconds in Preferences>Defaults>Clip Length.

VERTICAL VIDEO

The HERO7 cameras are the first GoPro cameras to offer the option to **record video in a Vertical Orientation**. Although traditional video has always been recorded in a landscape format, vertical video formats have risen in popularity out of the simple fact that we typically hold our phones in a vertical position.

To give users the option of recording vertical videos in-camera, the Hero7 can be set to rotate to a vertical format depending on the camera's orientation. Touch Screen items also rotate when the camera is rotated vertically.

If you like to record vertical videos, keep this feature enabled. However, **if you prefer to record videos in the traditional Landscape orientation,** *turn on Landscape Lock in the Touch Screen settings menu under Preferences>Touch Screen>Landscape Lock.* If you accidentally record vertical videos, you can easily rotate them in post-production, but it's easier to turn this function off if you don't need it.

One **creative use for vertical videos and time lapses** is to film a vertical 4k video (*Silver only) with intention of using keyframes to add a tilting effect (you will learn about keyframes in Step 5- Editing). When you edit the clip to 1080p, there is plenty of top to bottom area for adding a slow tilt. The tilt adds a lot of postproduction drama to a shot recorded without movement. When filming a vertical time lapse on the White (since the White can't film in 4k), edit your video to a 720p video, which is sufficient resolution for most social media.

TAKING PHOTOS

The HERO7 Silver and White not only record great videos, but the photos you can capture with these compact little cameras are super unique and characteristically "GoPro". Because of the versatility of GoPro cameras, there are a couple of ways you can set up your camera to take photos, from taking a single photo to taking a speedy burst of 15 photos in one second. The photo-taking capability of this camera is top-notch, and that is great motivation to understand how to get the most out of your Hero7 Silver or White for taking photos.

This section will help you understand when and how to use Photo Mode on the HERO7 Silver and White to capture the best photos possible.

PHOTO MODE

Photo Mode is designed for you to operate your HERO7 like a standard point and shoot camera, where pushing the Shutter Button tells your camera to take a photo. Taking a single photo in Photo Mode is perfect for high quality scenic photos or portraits.

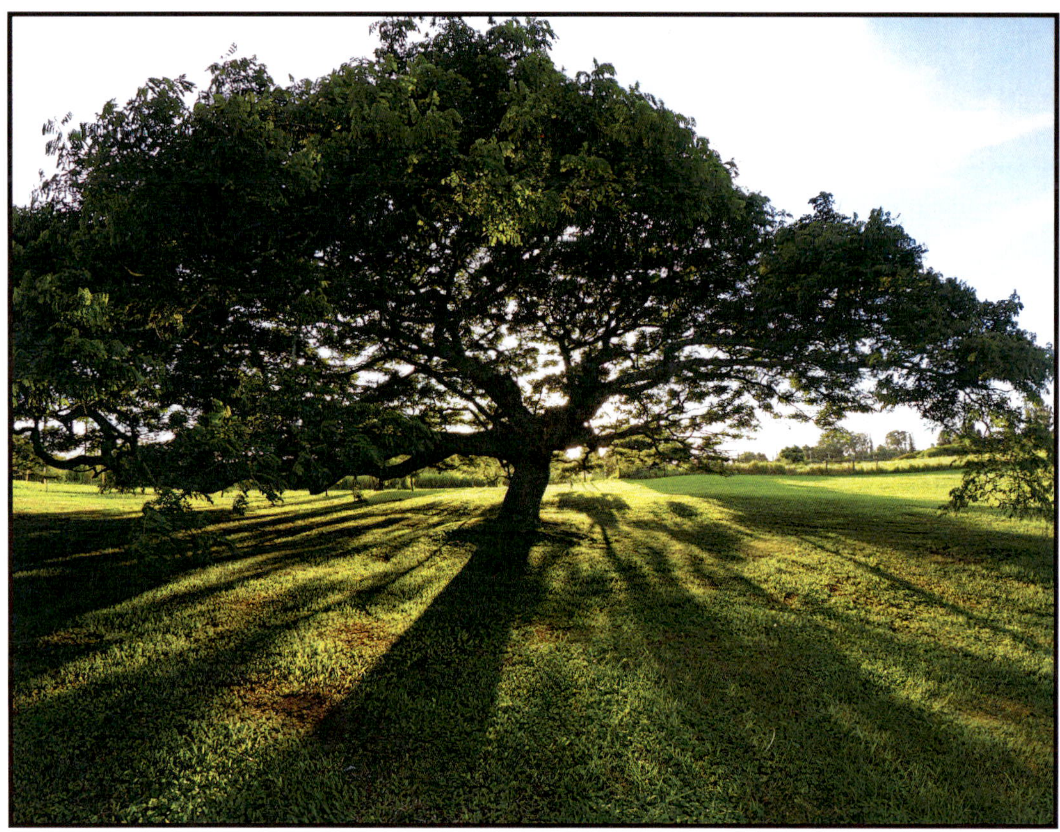

Photo taken with the HERO7 Silver camera in Photo Mode. The camera was handheld on the Shorty pole by GoPro. Colors were adjusted using the editing techniques in Step 5- Photo Editing.

Photo is your standard photo mode in which your camera takes one photo per push of the Shutter Button (or when you say, "GoPro Take A Photo"). Because your camera is only taking one photo, in certain situations, such as low might, photos taken in Photo Mode are noticeably higher quality than photos taken in Bursts (which you will learn about next). Photo mode is **best for shots that don't involve high action**, like a scenic photo or portrait.

When taking photos in Photo Mode, hold your camera steady and keep your subject around the middle of the frame for the least distortion. You can also rotate your camera 90 degrees to take vertical photos.

Your camera takes the photo immediately after you press the Shutter Button.

There are also two other options for capturing photos with your Hero7:

CONTINUOUS SHOOTING- Spur of the moment sequences

As an added feature, if you hold down the Shutter button, your camera will continuously take a sequence of up to 60 photos. This feature is useful when you want to **capture spur of the moment bursts of action**. When you don't have time to Tap the Burst icon, holding down the Shutter button gives you the freedom to snap a sequence anytime. You cannot use Voice Control to take continuous photos.

BURST- High Action Sports, Handheld Shots, Action Sequences

The other option for taking quick photo sequences is to Tap the Burst icon on the Touch Screen.

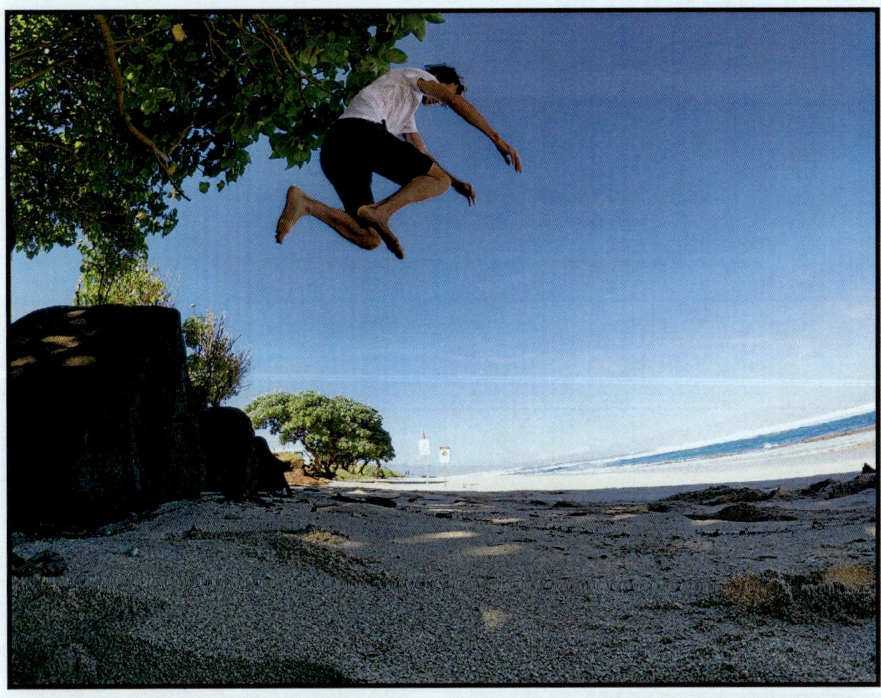

Photo taken with the HERO7 Silver camera in Burst Mode using the Self-Timer set to 10 seconds. The fast burst provided lots of photos to choose from to find that magic moment. The camera was mounted on a Joby GorillaPod mini tripod which was set on the sand.

Burst is **great for high action where timing is everything**. When Burst is turned on, your camera takes 15 photos in 1 second. Use Burst when shooting high action sports and choose the winning shot later. You won't miss a moment. This mode is best used when holding your camera and there are a few ways to press the Shutter Button to **capture yourself in action**. For some activities, the **Self-Timer set to 10 seconds** will give you enough time to press the Shutter and set yourself up for the shot. Press the Shutter Button on the camera or the GoPro App and let your camera shoot away. If you are close enough to your camera, say "GoPro Shoot Burst" to start shooting.

Burst photos can also be **used to make an action sequence**, where multiple photos of one subject are edited into a single frame. Combining the multiple images is not done automatically in the camera, but you can do this with photo-editing software (See Step 5- Editing an Action Sequence).

Because your camera takes a quick burst of photos in a short amount of time, when shooting Burst photos in low light, many will come out blurry. Usually you can pick out the best ones and come up with some usable photos. It is best, however, to **shoot Burst Mode photos in bright daylight** to give your camera enough light to produce in-focus photos. If you are filming in cloudy or shady conditions, 4k video is a better option for low light conditions. You can pull photos from the video, which you will learn how to do in Step 5.

WDR (*Silver Edition Only)

The HERO7 Silver automatically applies WDR (Wide Dynamic Range) to your photos. WDR improves the level of detail in an image's dark and bright areas. WDR is particularly effective for backlit scenes or scenes with a lot of contrast (dark and bright areas). WDR is applied automatically to all of your photos. Even though WDR produces more even-toned photos, adding contrast back into your photos when you edit (like you will learn about in Step 5- Photo Editing) will have a huge impact on the depth of your photos.

FOV TOUCH ZOOM

All Photo modes (including Continuous and Burst) offer the option of using Touch Zoom. Photos taken in photo modes are always captured at a 4:3 ratio and photos taken at any zoom level result in a 10 MP photo.

When zooming, you can see a live preview of your composition on the Touch Screen as you zoom in, which can be helpful to frame the best angle.

• When you use Touch Zoom in video, you can truly keep the same resolution because you are just using portion of the sensor. However, with photos, quality diminishes slightly as you zoom in, even though the result is a 3648px by 2736px photo in any field of view at any zoom level.

• You can also get a similar look to a zoomed in photo by cropping a Wide field of view photo and upsizing it if you need to. (We will get to that in Step 5-Creation).

• Some GoPro models offer a Linear field of view, which corrects the fisheye effect. If you want to remove the fisheye effect after the fact, you can easily replicate a Linear FOV when you edit. We will show you that also in Step 5-Creation- Removing Fisheye (for photos).

SELF-TIMER

In photo modes, self-timer can be **set to 3 or 10 seconds** which makes it easy to **capture the perfect selfie or scenic shot without any shake**. Self-timer is also useful to give yourself a few seconds between pressing the Shutter Button and checking your composition before the camera actually takes the photo.

Self-timer is useful for Burst photos to press the Shutter Button and give yourself 10 seconds to jump off a waterfall or whatever you like to do. Timing the 1 second burst of photos can be tricky, so it will probably take a few tries to get the shot. An easier alternative is to use the GoPro App to press the Shutter Button remotely. If you want to use Self-Timer when using the GoPro App, set the desired Self-Timer time on the camera first and then press the Shutter Button on the App.

To use Self Timer, press the Self-Timer Icon and select your desired timer time. When you take photo by pressing the Shutter Button, the self-timer begins counting down with the countdown time indicated on the back Touch Screen.

TIME LAPSE VIDEO

In Time Lapse Video Mode, your camera records one frame (similar to one photo) every .5 second. The individual frames are then **automatically stitched together** in the camera and **played back as a video** at 30 frames per second. Because the frames are spaced apart and then played back quickly at 15x the normal speed, there are gaps in between moments and time appears to speed up, creating the time lapse effect.

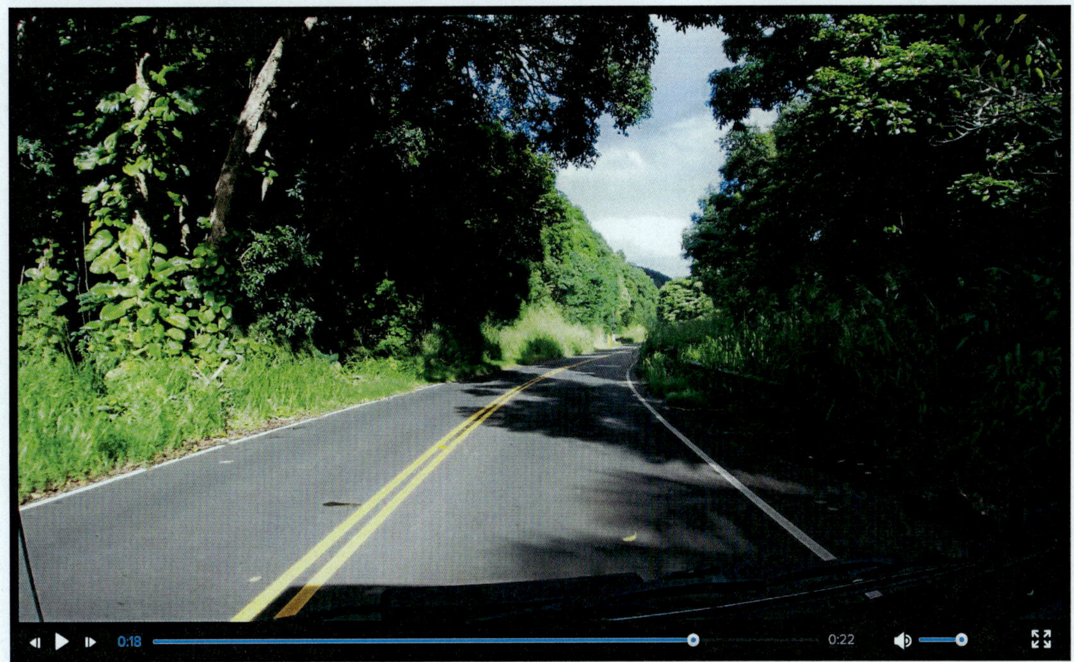

Shot on the HERO7 Silver in Time Lapse Video Mode in 4k. The camera was mounted on the Suction Cup Mount to the windshield as shown in Step 3- Mounting.

GO DEEPER

This section will help you with some of the more technical aspects of Time Lapse Video Mode.

• The time counter will **display the playback duration of the video**, not the recording time. To **capture one second of video, you need to record 30 frames**. The time counter will remain at 00:01 (1 second) until you have recorded 30 frames (which takes 15 seconds).

• In Time Lapse Video Mode **on the Hero7 Silver**, there are **two resolutions available**: **4k** is for 16:9 Widescreen shots in Wide FOV. Turn 4k off for Standard Aspect Ratio shots in **1440p**. On the White, all time lapse videos are recorded at 1440p.

• **Battery runtime** in Time Lapse Video Mode is similar to recording normal video in the same resolution (either 4k or 1440p on the Silver) even though you are capturing far fewer frames.

Time lapses make an artsy addition to a video. Learning the art of creating a visually-appealing time lapse takes some experimentation to get right, so don't be discouraged if you don't get a great one on your first try. The **following tips will help you with some of the more creative aspects of recording a memorable time lapse:**

• The Hero7 Silver and White only has one interval setting, which is 15x (1 frame every .5 second)

• A **short interval** (like what is available on the Hero7 Silver/White) works well for a scene with **continuously moving action** like waves lapping on the beach or traffic in a city for example. A short interval is also useful for **an event that happens over a relatively short period of time**, like a sunrise or preparing your gear to go ride.

• The short interval setting does not work as well for a scene where there is **not a lot of movement**, like slow-moving clouds, or for **longer duration events**, like road trips, construction or long art projects. If you film longer duration events, you will need to speed up the action when you edit the video.

• For a still time lapse, use a tripod or set your camera in a stationary position so the scene creates the movement instead of your camera. Any movement of your camera will be intensified. See more tips in the time lapse section in Step 4- Capture Your Action.

For more time lapse tips and ideas, see the time lapse section in Step 4- Capture Your Action!

ADVANCED VIDEO & PHOTO SETTING OPTIONS

After you familiarize yourself with your new camera and become comfortable with the basic operations, you may want to utilize the following setting options for specific shooting needs. The following setting options can be utilized when recording videos or photos.

EXPOSURE CONTROL / SPOT METER

Exposure Control allows you to **specify a particular area of the frame to determine exposure**. This is especially useful for high contrast scenes, for example if part of the scene is in complete shade and the other area is in bright sunlight. Your camera naturally tries to set an exposure that balances the two extremes. With Exposure Control, you can tell it to expose for the shady area, or just the bright area.

There are two options for Exposure Control- one, called Auto Exposure (or Spot Meter for the center of the frame), is to continually set exposure based on a particular area of the image. When you move your camera, the exposure will change as the lighting changes in that region. The second option, called Locked Exposure, allows you to set the exposure based on a certain area of the image, then lock that exposure until you deactivate it, or switch modes.

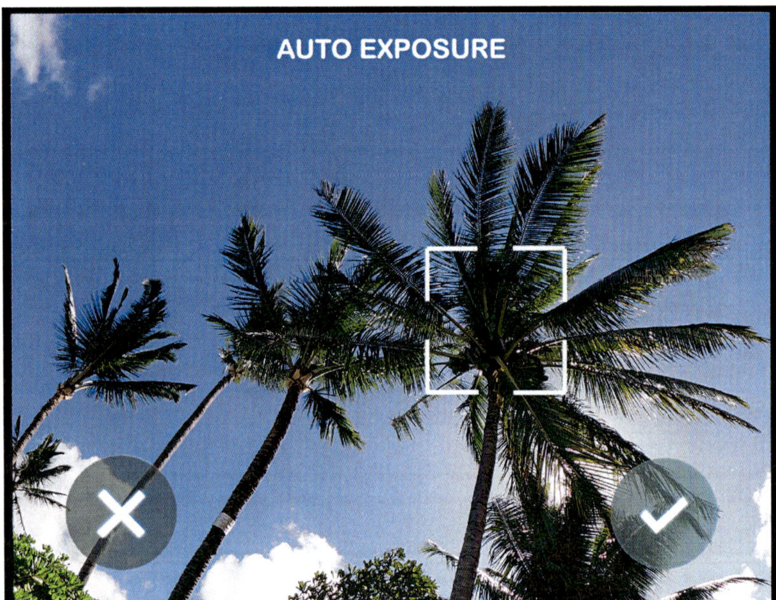

To activate Auto Exposure or Locked Exposure:

1. Press the Touch Screen until a box appears and then shrinks to the area where you are pressing.
2. Drag the box to the area where you would like to determine exposure. Or tap another area of the frame.
3. If you are using Locked Exposure, tap inside the Auto Exposure box to change it to Locked Exposure.
4. Click the check box to enable Exposure Control.

Exposure Control can be disabled by changing modes, turning off your camera, or pressing the screen and tapping the "x".

PREFERENCES

The Dashboard and Preferences Menu allows you to change various settings on your camera.

After powering on your camera, Swipe Down on the Touch Screen to bring up the Dashboard with the Preferences Options. Some of these options, such as Voice Control, QuikCapture, Connections, and checking your camera's firmware version were discussed in Step 1.

You can come back to revisit most of these settings once you are comfortable using your camera. Two of the settings, Date and PAL/NTSC, should be checked now, but the rest can wait until you begin using your camera. If you have not done so yet, **start by setting the date** so you can keep your files organized. Also, if you are outside of North America, check to see if your camera is set to PAL or NTSC.

SCREEN LOCK

With the Dashboard open, the Screen Lock option is the fourth button at the right of the Touch Screen. When Screen Lock is enabled, the Touch Screen locks automatically to **prevent settings from accidentally changing** or to prevent Exposure Control from being set (which happens sometimes when water gets on the Touch Screen). This is especially useful when you are going in the water or when carrying your camera in your pocket. To unlock Screen Lock, tap on the screen, Swipe Down and then tap on the lock. This will allow you to make changes before the screen automatically locks again.

The following options are found in the Preferences Menu.

DEFAULTS

Clip Length

When you press the Clip Icon in Video Mode on the Touch Screen, this defines your default clip to either 15 or 30 seconds.

 **Mode**

This defines which capture mode you want to be available when you turn your camera on. The **default is Video Mode/Video**, but if you find that you are using a different mode most the time, set your preference here.

GENERAL SETTINGS

 **Beep Volume**

This allows you to **adjust the volume of the beeps to High, Medium, Low or completely silent (Mute)**. The beeps are helpful to let you know if your camera stops recording when your camera is mounted out of sight, on your helmet for example.

If you are recording nature or music, the beeps tend to be loud and distracting so you may want to lower the volume or turn them off completely. To quickly mute the beeps, press the Beeps Button at the top of the Dashboard.

 **Auto Power OFF**

If you find that you keep forgetting to turn off your camera and the battery dies before you get a chance to use your camera, you can **set your camera to shut off automatically** after 5, 15 or 30 minutes of inactivity, or Never. **15 minutes is a good option** to prevent an accidental dead battery since it can be difficult to tell when your camera is turned on.

 **LED Lights**

You can **control the amount of LED lights that light up** on your camera. The options are All On, All Off, or Front Off Only. The LED lights flash while videoing or taking photos. The lights are pretty small, but sometimes if you are filming close to your subject, the red glow from the LED lights can show up on your subject. Also, if you are recording video at night, turn off the LED lights if they are affecting your scene.

 **Date /Time**

Set the date on your camera. If you have any hope of staying organized with the huge number of files produced by a GoPro camera, you need to be able to search through your files by date. So, before you record any more footage, go into the Preferences Menu and make sure the date is correct. When you connect your camera to the GoPro App or Quik for Desktop, the date will set automatically.

TOUCH SCREEN

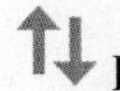 **Landscape Lock**

With this setting, you can **lock the camera to a Landscape Orientation** so it will records in landscape orientation only. This is useful if you don't want to record Vertical Videos.

When Landscape Lock is turned Off, your camera will automatically adjust to the correct orientation including a vertical orientation. After rotating your camera, make sure the camera has changed to correct orientation by looking at the Touch Screen icons to make sure they are in the correct orientation. The orientation is based on the beginning of your video clip and once you start recording, the orientation is locked.

 **Screensaver and Brightness**

This option allows you to change the settings for the Touch Screen on the back of your camera.

Under the Screensaver option, you can set the Touch Screen to sleep after 1, 2, or 3 minutes or never. Setting the display to sleep after a short period will help to maximize the battery life but may cause the screen to sleep while you are filming longer clips. If you are using the Touch Screen to compose your shots as you film, set the Touch Screen to shut off after 3 minutes or never, depending on the length of your shots.

You can also adjust the Brightness of the Touch Screen to suit your tastes. Plus, a lower brightness uses less battery.

REGIONAL MENU

 **GPS (*Silver Only)**

When GPS is enabled, your camera will record key GPS stats, which can be used to show gauges (Speed, Path, G-Force, etc.) in Quik for Desktop, show speed in Quik, or for geotagging your photos.

Language

Use this dialog to change your camera's display language.

 **Video Format**

If you are in North America, film in NTSC. If you are outside of North America, most televisions outside of North America use PAL, so set your camera to PAL. Setting your camera to PAL will affect the frame rates as shown in the video settings section.

RESET

Format SD Card

After you transfer footage to your computer, select Format SD Card to erase all of the files.

Congratulations, you've made it through the settings step.

You are now ready to move on to Step 3 where you will learn how to mount your camera!

STEP THREE

MOUNTING

Set Up Your Camera To Work The Angles

The quality that really makes GoPro cameras stand out is their ability to be mounted in unique locations to capture angles that used to be unwieldy or nearly impossible. When it comes to mounting your HERO7, think outside the box. Look for angles you've never seen before. Or use others as inspiration to record your life in a way you never thought to do before. **Getting creative with mounts is what will make your footage truly unique.**

There are hundreds of ways to mount your HERO7 and the possibilities keep expanding as creative users come up with new mounts and new mounting techniques. If there is an angle you can imagine, there is a way to capture it with your HERO7. And the best part is that this camera is so small and lightweight that it's hardly even noticeable as you carry it along with you on your big (and small) adventures.

So study up and learn how these mounts work so you can decide which ones will best capture your point of view. The mounting examples also provide more insight into choosing your modes and settings for particular shots.

This chapter begins with **the basic elements- the camera, the frame and buckles**- and then gets deeper into the wide variety of mounts you can use with your HERO7 to get the angles you want to capture.

Other companies besides GoPro make versions of many of these mounts, however this book only points out other available options when they offer something unique from the original GoPro mounts. If you do buy a third party mount, make sure to check the quality before you trust it in high-impact situations as some of the cheaper options can break easily.

GETTING STARTED

Your HERO7 is **part of a unique mounting system** that made GoPro cameras stand apart from other cameras in the first place. Your **camera** is inserted into the **frame** which can be attached to a variety of **mounts** using a **thumbscrew**. This basic combination is the starting point for a whole world of fun, creative mounting techniques.

Let's get started with one of the most exciting and creative aspects of using your HERO7- mounting!

ACTIVITY LEGEND

As you learn about each mount, you will see the following icons which are shown to recommend which activities each mount is most useful for.

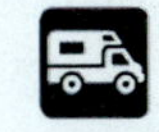
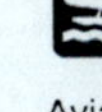
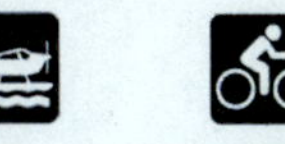

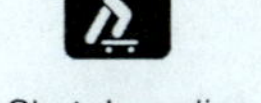

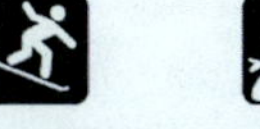

Auto/Trucks — Aviation — Bike — Boat — Diving/ Snorkeling — Rock Climbing — Skateboarding — Skiing — Snowboarding — Standup Paddling

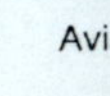

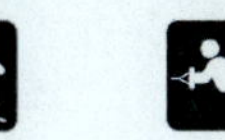
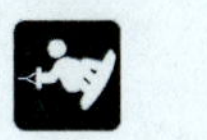

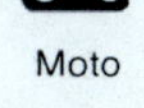

Fishing — Hang Gliding/ Paragliding — Hiking — Kayaking/ Canoeing — Moto — Surfing — Wakeboarding — Windsurfing — Kitesurfing

MOUNTING YOUR CAMERA

THE HERO7 CAMERA

YES, THE CAMERA IS WATERPROOF!

The HERO7 camera is **waterproof to 33' (10m) without an additional case**. For years, earlier generations of GoPro cameras had to be inserted into a waterproof case to create a waterproof camera set up.

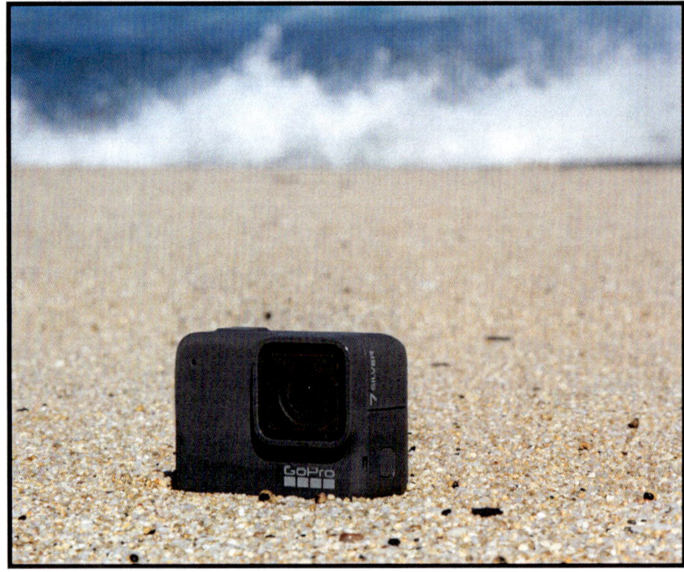

With the HERO7, your camera is always ready to get wet! The HERO7 cannot go as deep as earlier GoPro cameras which required a separate waterproof housing, but 33' (10m) is deep enough for most activities besides scuba diving. If you want to go deeper, you will need a **GoPro model that is compatible with the SuperSuit**, which can withstand up to 196ft (60m) of depth. Unfortunately, the Hero 7 Silver/White is not compatible with the SuperSuit.

As long as the side door is securely closed, the HERO7 camera itself is always ready for the water. You don't need to worry about it. This means there are no cases to worry about and no prep to get your camera ready to film in the water.

Whenever you finish accessing the side door and are ready to start using your camera again, **make sure the door is closed completely with the Latch Release tab flush to the camera**. You'll notice a small rubber gasket around the opening. That gasket keeps water out of your camera. Keeping the door securely closed is essential to keeping your camera waterproof.

When your camera is new, the door should close easily and securely latch. But after time, some dust or dirt may accumulate making it a little rougher to close. Make sure to keep any sand or dirt off the gasket by cleaning it periodically.

CARING FOR YOUR CAMERA

There are a few simple steps you can take to keep your camera working like new for years:

• **Rinse off your camera and mounts with fresh water** after using them in the ocean or getting them dirty. Gently dry your camera with a soft cloth and **blow off the residual water around the door** before opening it.

• The glass piece directly over the lens of your camera is called a "lens port." **Avoid touching the lens port with your fingers.** You don't want grease, sunblock, or scratches on the lens port. Make sure your lens port is always clean! This is your camera's window to the world. The flat lens port that comes on the HERO7 **works great for clear, in-focus shots underwater and on land**, as long as it is clean. The lens cover on the Hero7 is not replaceable so be careful not to scratch or damage it.

• **If you are in the water**, water drops on the lens port quickly ruin a shot. **To prevent water drops from collecting on the front of your lens port when your housing gets wet, lick the lens port** and let it dry before you get in the water. When you get in the water, dip the camera to give it a quick rinse. This is an old surf photographer trick and it works really well to prevent water from beading up into visible drops on the lens port. You may need to lick the lens port a few times during your session and dip the camera underwater often. Although GoPro recommends it, don't use Rain-X on the outside because this makes water bead up and get in the way of your shot.

FOGGING ISSUES

• Since the HERO7 doesn't require a separate waterproof housing, fogging (moisture on the inside of the lens) is not a major problem, but **some condensation can occur under the lens port in humid environments**. If you notice excessive fogging under the lens port, stop recording when it is convenient to let the camera cool down. As the camera cools off, you will notice that the moisture inside of the glass will start to dry out. The fogging is **caused by the difference in temperature** inside of the glass and outside, just like a car window fogs up. You can minimize this by letting your camera adjust to the climate. For example, if you come out of an air-conditioned room into 100-degree heat, wait a bit for the air inside the camera to adjust. If you are going into the ocean or lake, put the camera underwater for a minute to let the temperature adjust.

• If you are experiencing fogging problems during a filming session, try to record only when you need to. **Use QuikCapture** to reduce standby time, which will allow your camera to cool off in between shots giving the moisture time to dissipate.

• After the session, **rinse off your camera**, dry it well and **leave your camera to dry out with the side door open** to let any moisture escape. If you are having a repetitive problem with moisture, put your camera in a sealed Ziploc bag along with some pennies (copper is said to be antifungal) wrapped in a couple of dry washcloths fresh from the dryer. Open the camera door and leave the camera in the bag overnight to extract the moisture.

A FEW MORE MOUNTING TIPS

Keep it simple. You could get overambitious and buy every mount (because yes, there is a fun, creative use for almost every mount), but simplicity is going to be your best friend. When you are out having fun, whether it's biking, snowboarding, or just cruising around, the key is to be in the moment. Prepare beforehand. Select two or three mounts max to take with you to avoid spending your time fumbling around setting up the camera. The magic is in the moment, so have your camera ready and film the best you can with what you have...which leads to the next filming tip....

Put effort into your shots. Even though they might just look like shoot-from-the hip style shots, most of the impactful GoPro videos or photos you see took effort. Select a few mounts for each activity and keep it simple, but once you start filming, put your energy into getting "the shot", not just a bunch of average shots. This may mean you need to walk closer to your subject, or pause a moment longer, but the images you create will reflect your energy. There is a huge difference between "I could have taken that shot" and "I took that shot." With the latter, the proof is in the image.

THE FRAME

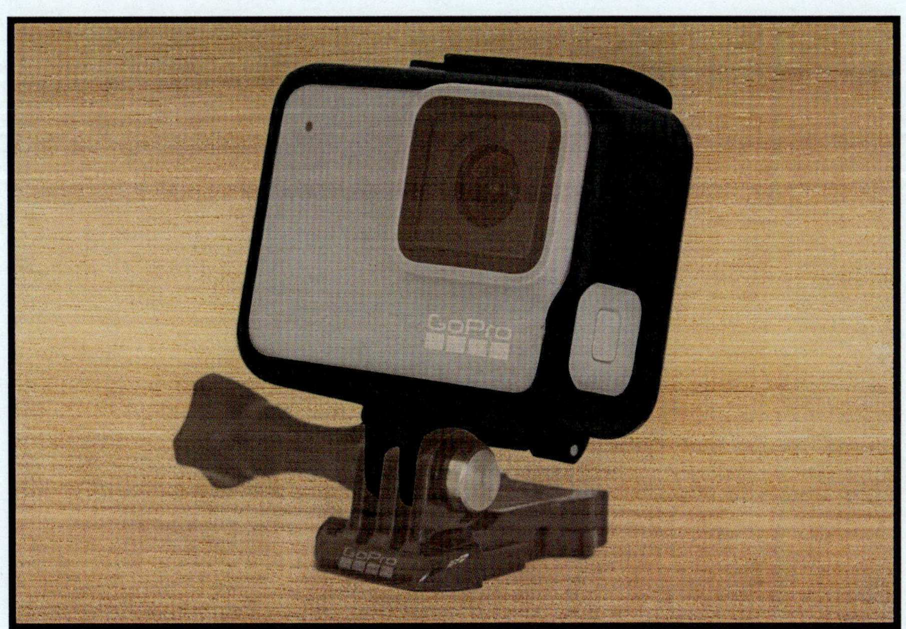

The HERO7 comes mounted in a "frame". The Frame holds your camera securely allowing you to mount it to a variety of mounts using a thumbscrew. When your camera is mounted in the Frame, the microphones are open for clear audio, especially in low-speed situations.

TIPS FOR USING THE FRAME

• To insert your camera into the frame, **lift the tab on top** of the frame to release the backdoor. Lower the backdoor and **slide your camera into the frame from the back**. Close the backdoor, **hooking the latch onto the backdoor before closing it**. Always **make sure the latch on the Frame is completely closed all the way across** when getting ready for any extreme activities. It is a common mistake for the latch to grab the lip of the housing on one side, but not be fully latched all the way across.

• The Frame **can be used with any of the buckles** or attached directly to some mounts. Use the **long Thumbscrew to connect the Frame to a mount**. A short Thumbscrew only needs to be used when connecting any additional mounting pieces together.

• **Keep the Shutter Button at the top or bottom of your desired frame** if you want to record horizontally-framed videos. If you forget to orientate your camera correctly, you will record a vertical video, which is great for photos and fine for videos as long as it's intentional. Use Landscape Lock in the Preferences>Touch Screen Menu if you prefer landscape videos.

• If you remove the side door cover, you can **access the side ports** to charge the battery, transfer files or connect to external USB power while your camera is still in the frame. However, **your camera is NOT waterproof with the door removed**. Be careful removing the side door because it breaks easily.

• The HERO7, like all GoPro cameras, **does NOT float. Whenever you are going in the water, make sure you use a Floaty Backdoor or a floating handle** to float your camera. A floating handle is the best option if you are holding your camera so you can still view the Touch Screen. Otherwise, use a Floaty when your camera is mounted to your equipment and lock the Touch Screen to prevent water from changing the settings. Since the HERO7 Silver/White doesn't have a front display screen, select your settings before closing the Floaty Backdoor and use the front indicator light and beeps to make sure the camera is recording. The Floaty attaches to the backdoor of the Frame (the Floaty comes with a solid backdoor) to **float your HERO7** in case your setup accidentally comes out of a mount in the water. You don't want to watch your camera sink out of your hands and into the depths!

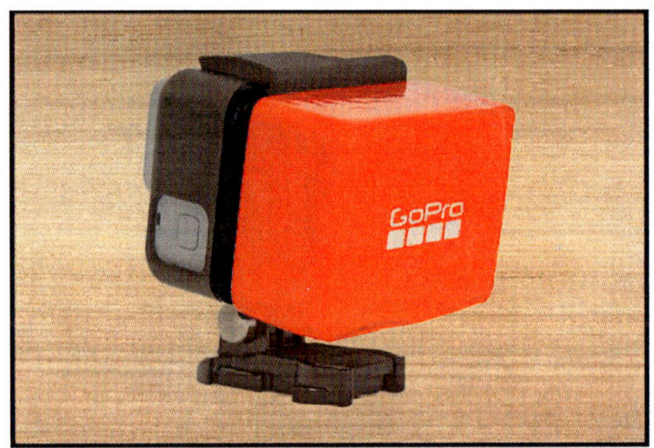

The Floaty Backdoor

THUMBSCREW BASICS

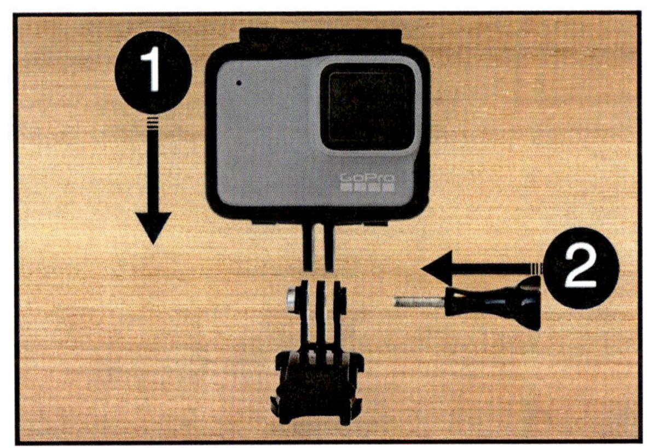

Your HERO7 attaches to mounts using a thumbscrew. Although this is a simple step, there are a couple basics you should know about connecting your camera using a thumbscrew.

• **Secure your angle**, especially for extreme sports! Once you have figured out exactly how you want the camera pointing, **use a Philips screwdriver** to tighten any thumbscrews that hold the camera in place. If you don't tighten the screws properly, especially when you are in water, the camera can accidentally rotate and you won't know if you are still capturing the right angle. Even small bumps and shakes can move your camera around very easily, so use a screwdriver to tighten the thumbscrews as tight as you can. Alternatively, GoPro makes the Tool, which is used to tighten thumbscrews and fits into your pocket better than a screwdriver.

• You can **use an extension arm or section** with many of the mounts to capture unique perspectives. An extension arm can be used to lift your camera up from a low position or to move your camera out and away from a helmet or board. Using an extension on a helmet tends to feel awkward because of the weight, but it can produce some unique perspectives. A rotating swivel mount on top of your helmet is one of the most interesting helmet shots using an extension.

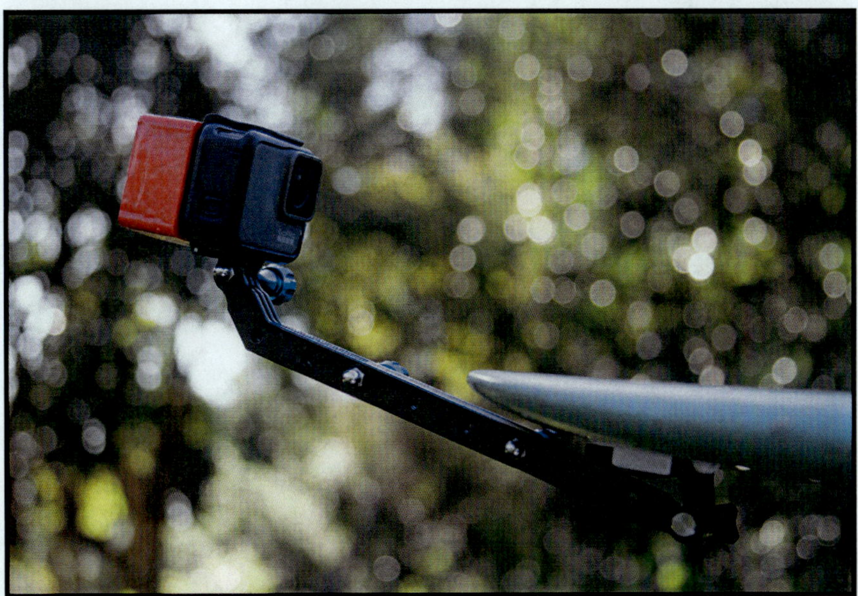

The Smatree Aluminum Arm mounted to a Surfboard Mount on the front of a longboard surfboard adds enough distance to record the entire board in the shot.

The Smatree Aluminum Arm, the SP Gadgets section or the GoPole Arm are a few of the best premade extensions.

BUCKLES

Many of the mounts in this step require that you use a "Buckle" to slide your HERO7 Silver or White into the mount.

As you just saw, your camera is attached to a buckle using a long thumbscrew. The **buckle then slides into the mount**, locking your camera in place.

There are **three buckle options to choose from** when mounting your camera on a mount base and each has its benefits. The Mounting Buckle comes with your HERO7. The other two buckles are included with other mounts as you expand your mounting options.

TIPS FOR USING THE BUCKLES

• The buckles can be inserted into the mount bases **facing either direction**.

• Except for the Swivel Buckle, your camera can't rotate in the buckle. You can **add extensions to the other buckles** if you need to change the orientation of your camera. A 3-Way Pivot Arm can be used to rotate the camera 90 degrees, so if you are just looking for more height but want your camera to point the same direction, you will need to use two extension pieces. Make sure to **tighten each joint** so there is no weak point in your setup.

• **Vertical Mounting.** If you want to mount your GoPro for a vertical composition, you may need some additional mounting pieces. Some mounts, such as the Suction Cup or Jaws Flex Clamp, allow you to rotate the camera on the mount. But for a horizontal mount, such as a tripod or an adhesive mount on a surfboard, use the Helmet Side Mount pieces to rotate your camera vertically.

• After inserting the buckle into a mount, push down the **attached black locking plug** to secure your mount in place. This prevents the buckle from accidentally releasing from the mount. The locking plug also helps to reduce vibrations.

MOUNTING BUCKLE

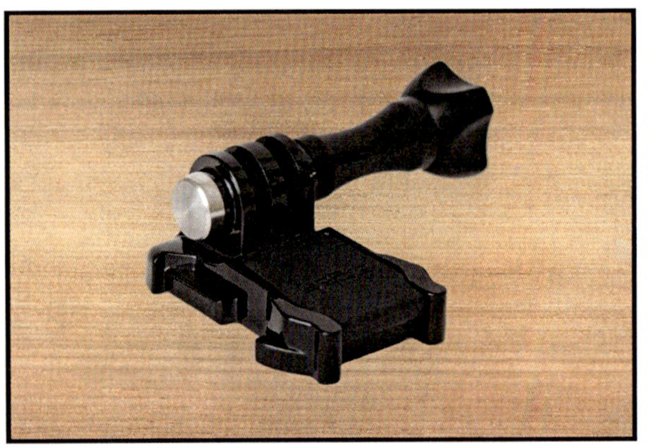

The Mounting Buckle is **for low-profile mounting positions** where you don't need a lot of front to back rotation to get the angle you are looking for. Because of its limited range of motion, this buckle works best for horizontal surfaces. With its low-profile, this buckle provides a securely mounted position that **can handle a lot of impact** for extreme moments.

VERTICAL MOUNTING BUCKLE

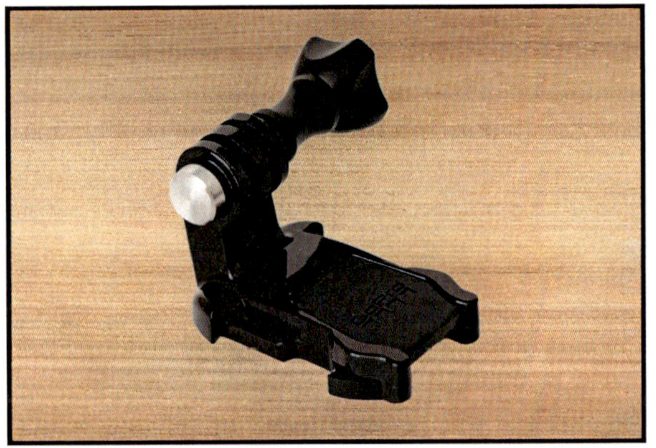

The Vertical Mounting Buckle allows for a **greater range of motion than the Mounting Buckle**. When using this buckle, you can rotate your camera 180 degrees from front to back.

The Vertical Mounting Buckle is usually the best option for vertical mounting positions. Because the Frame mounts from the bottom, this buckle provides an easy way to mount your camera vertically, either right side up or upside down. However, the name "Vertical Mounting Buckle" is somewhat confusing because this buckle is not only used for vertical mounting positions. You can also use this buckle on a horizontal surface for a little extra distance from the mounting surface and a greater tilting range.

Range of Motion
using the Vertical Buckle

SWIVEL BUCKLE

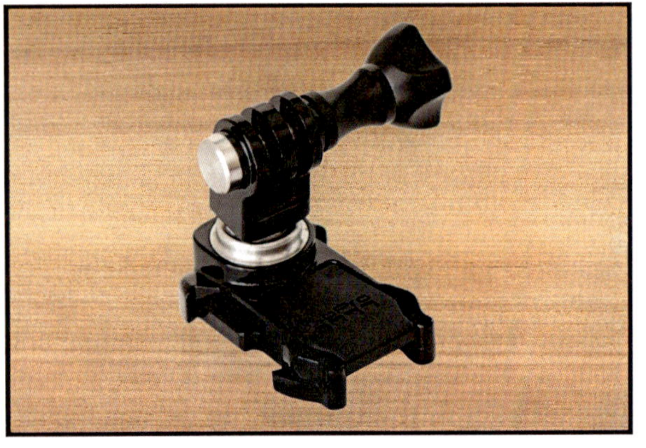

The Swivel Buckle/Mount **can be tilted 30 degrees in any direction**, which allows you to fine tune your angles when your camera is already mounted. The Swivel Buckle also allows you to turn your camera around completely, which makes it easy to capture different angles from one mounting position. The Swivel Buckle is a bit tricky to adjust because the joint is tight, which is needed to prevent accidental slipping.

• Use this buckle **if you need to make minor adjustments to straighten the camera's angle** after the camera is mounted.

• When the Swivel Buckle is used **for helmet mounting positions**, this compact camera setup can be adjusted easily for a straight horizon.

• The Swivel Buckle is not the best choice for extreme sports because the buckle can move when knocked.

ADHESIVE MOUNTS

When properly applied, Adhesive Mounts are **the most secure base for mounting your camera to most surfaces**. The Adhesive Mounts stick to smooth surfaces using a super strong adhesive tape. They are single use and can be removed, but they are **typically left on for more permanent use**. It is especially important to follow the mounting instructions if you are using the mount in cold weather. The following tips will help you use the Adhesive Mounts to their full potential.

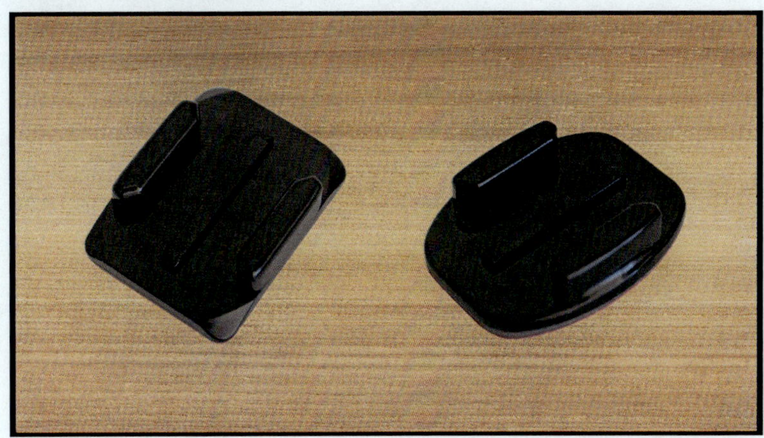

TIPS FOR USING ADHESIVE MOUNTS

- **Do not apply the mounts to a flexible surface**, like the nose of a snowboard. The mount can come off when the surface flexes.

- To **remove a mount** from a tough surface, you can usually pry it off with a butter knife. If you are worried about damaging the surface, use a hairdryer to soften the adhesive and slowly peel it off.

- When setting up a new angle, the best option is to **always use a new mount**. If you must reuse a mount, make sure to use a new piece of adhesive tape. **3M VHB 4991** is the super strong adhesive bonding tape that comes on GoPro® mounts. You can pick up a roll online and it's always good to have on hand if you plan to reuse any mounts. To reuse a mount, peel off the old adhesive and stick on the new mounting tape. If the mounting tape is in strips that are narrower than the mount, use multiple strips as close together as possible. Then trim the excess using scissors.

- When possible, use a camera tether for backup.

- Adhesive mounts can withstand temperatures up to 250°F (121°C).

- When mounting your camera, **make sure the buckle "clicks" into place** to lock it into the mount.

ADHESIVE MOUNT MOUNTING INSTRUCTIONS:

Follow these steps to securely mount your camera using an adhesive mount:

1. First check to **make sure you are using the right adhesive mount** for the surface you are mounting to. If you are mounting to a flat surface, use the Flat Adhesive Mount or Surfboard Mount. When mounting to a curved surface, use the Curved Adhesive Mount. Before removing the backing from the adhesive, test the mounting position to make sure the edges of the mount sit flush on the surface.

2. Use isopropyl alcohol to **clean the surface** where you are going to place the mount. Make sure there is no wax or sand on the surface. Let the alcohol dry or wipe clean before moving to the next step.

3. Decide which direction you want the camera to face when mounted and **make sure the groove for the camera to slide into faces that direction**. You can insert the camera forwards or backwards, but you can't easily rotate the camera once it is mounted.

4. The mount works **best if applied at room temperature**. Peel the paper backing from the mount and stick the mount to the surface. NOTE: The adhesive does not feel extremely sticky to the touch and needs to be pressed hard onto the mounting surface. For tricky surfaces, use a hair dryer to heat up the red plastic liner that covers the adhesive before removing it. This will make the adhesive tackier and improve the adhesion. Some people use a lighter to soften the adhesive, but be careful not to burn it.

5. For the strongest bond, **wait 24 hours before placing your camera into the mount** to let the adhesive form a strong bond. After 72 hours, the mount will be fully set to the surface.

CURVED ADHESIVE MOUNT

   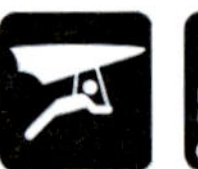 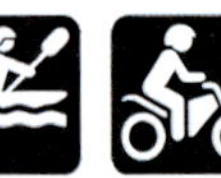    

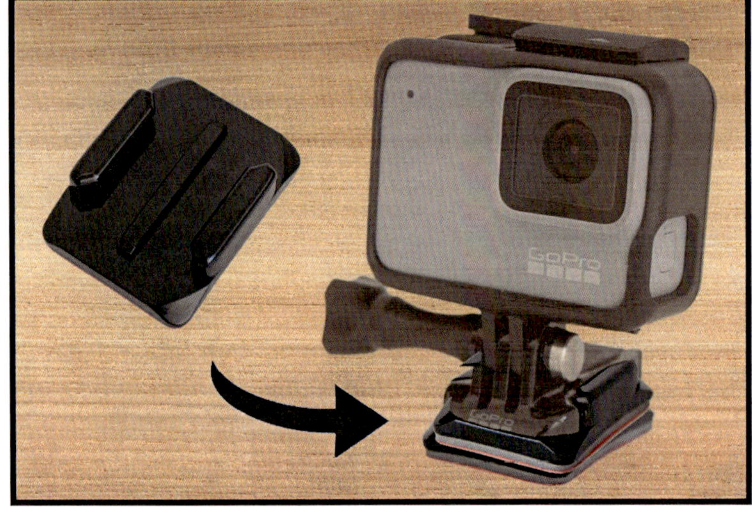

The Curved Adhesive Mount has a slightly curved base **for mounting to rounded objects**, most commonly a helmet or a curved surface of a vehicle. The Curved Adhesive Mount can be easily distinguished from the Flat Adhesive Mount by its square corners.

MOUNTING TIPS:

• Follow the Adhesive Mount Mounting Instructions in the beginning of the Adhesive Mount Section to set up a secure mount.

• When using this mount on a helmet, **find the best position and curve to match the base of the mount**. Inspect all the edges of the mount to make sure you have a good fit. If the edges of the mount lift slightly because the curve of the mount doesn't match the curve of your helmet, you can secure it using a small amount of epoxy or sun-curing surfboard resin (like Solarez). Make sure to only apply the resin around the base of the mount, not on the part of the mount where the camera slides in.

• This is the best mounting base to use for mounting your GoPro on a helmet. See the Helmet Mounting Tips in the Helmet and Wearable Mounts section for more ideas on where to use this mount for Helmet Cam angles.

MOUNTING EXAMPLE:

MOUNTED ON TOP OF A HELMET

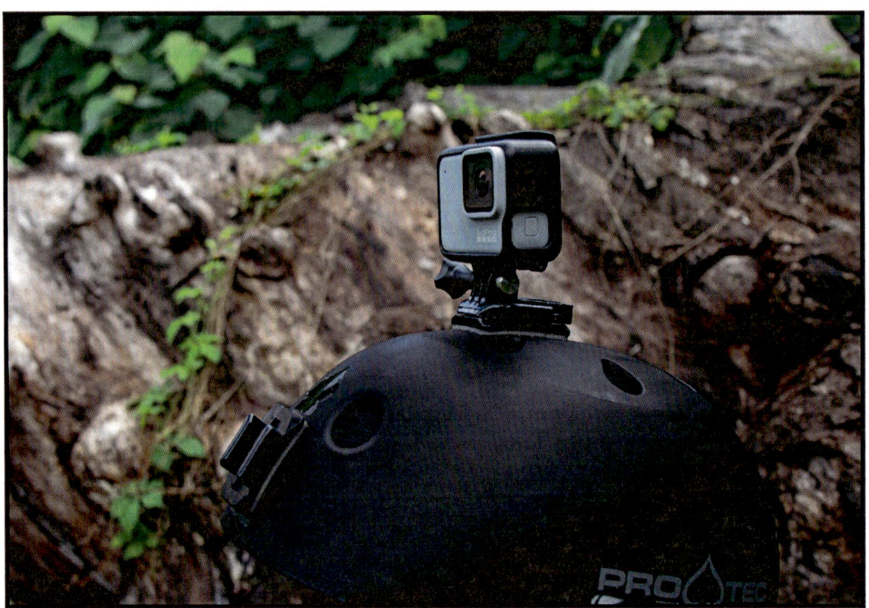

• When riding a bike or other vehicle, this angle captures a forward view of your action but is difficult to include your body in the frame. The Helmet Front Mount is a better option if you want to capture more of your handlebars in the shot.

• You can easily flip the camera around 180 degrees for a rear-facing view.

FLAT ADHESIVE MOUNT

   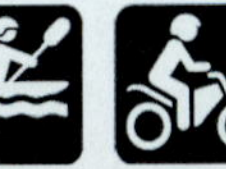 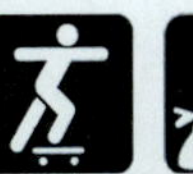   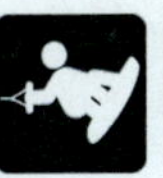 

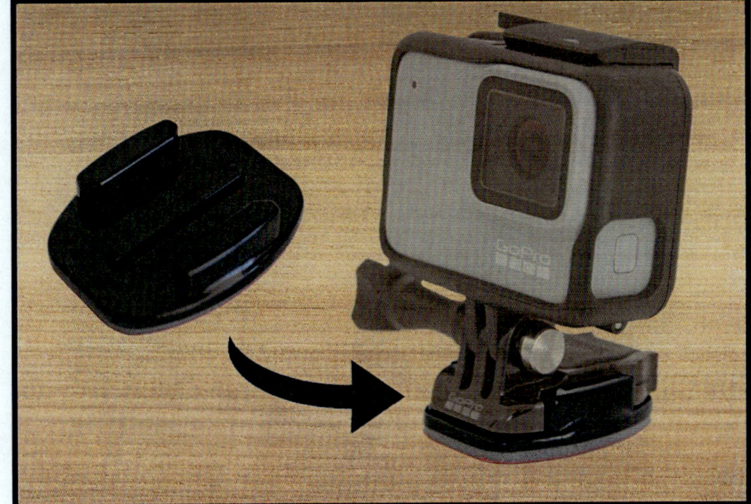

The Flat Adhesive Mount is a simple, low-profile mount **for flat, non-flexible surfaces**. The Flat Mount has a flat base and rounded corners. When mounted properly to a flat surface, this mount provides a secure, semi-permanent base to hold your camera. The best application for the Flat Adhesive Mount is to a location where you can use the mount repeatedly- e.g. your own car, plane, boat, or sporting equipment.

MOUNTING TIPS:

• Follow the Adhesive Mount Mounting Instructions in the beginning of the Adhesive Mount Section to set up a secure mount. The mount is very unlikely to fall off if mounted as instructed on a non-flexible surface.

• **Drilled Mount.** For a secure mount in applications where a typical adhesive mount might come off, you can **modify the mount so that it can be drilled into a surface**. To do this: 1) Drill a hole in the middle of the mount, 2) Countersink a hole for the head of the screw (so it doesn't interfere with your camera sliding on) and 3) Screw or bolt your mount onto your board, surface, etc.

• The **Surfboard Mount** is a flat adhesive mount with **more surface area** than the standard Flat Adhesive Mount. It comes with a separate tether mount that fits together snugly with the cutout on the Surfboard Mount. The extra surface area creates a stronger bond, and along with the included tether mount, this mount is a safe bet for holding onto your camera, even in big surf. To put your camera into the Surfboard Mount, **with the tether attached to your camera, insert the tether through the tether mount first**. Then, loop the tether over your camera to form a loop at the tether mount. Your camera will fit through even with a Floaty. Finally, **slide your camera** into the Surfboard Mount.

• Do not use an Adhesive Mount on a **SoftTop surfboard or bodyboard**. If you are riding a SoftTop surfboard or a bodyboard, **use the GoPro Bodyboard Mount** instead.

• Removable Instrument Mounts can be used repeatedly for a more temporary mounting option. The adhesive as not as secure and can be removed easily.

MOUNTING EXAMPLE:

<u>SURFBOARD MOUNT ON THE NOSE OF A SURFBOARD</u>

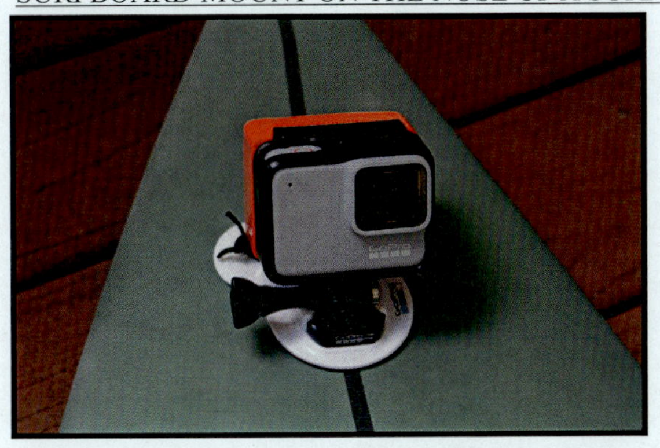

• The HERO7 White is shown mounted in the Surfboard Mount. The Floaty was used on the Frame to float the camera in the rare event that the mount was pulled off the board. The Touch Screen was locked to prevent water from accidentally changing settings since it's not visible behind the Floaty Backdoor. Remember to select your settings before closing the Floaty Backdoor.

• When your camera is mounted at foot level and close to you, **angle the camera back in the mount** to capture more of the subject and less surfboard in the foreground.

OTHER AVAILABLE VERSIONS:

• K-Edge's Go Big GoPro Adapter Mount comes with two counter sunk holes so you can screw your mount onto any surface you drill holes into.

• BRLS Removable Suction Cup Surfboard Mount- Three suction cups attach the mount securely to any surfboard or clean, flat surface and can be easily removed. This is a non-adhesive alternative to the Surfboard Mount which is a great option when you are using someone else's surfboard.

CAMERA TETHER MOUNT

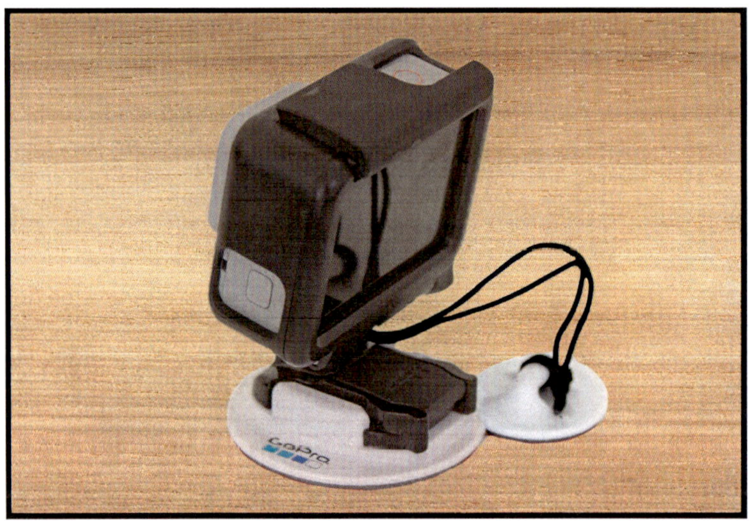

A Camera Tether Mount is a separate adhesive mount with a lanyard/leash that attaches to the camera to **provide backup in case the primary mount fails**. You can use camera tethers anywhere you can apply an adhesive mount. The adhesive mounts are unlikely to come off if applied correctly, but it's reassuring to know your camera will still be attached (albeit flapping around) if the primary mount fails.

If the primary mount does fail and the camera tether is holding your camera, you will want to stop whatever you are doing as soon as possible to prevent damage to your camera or the surface it is attached to.

MOUNTING TIPS:

• Find a flat spot on whatever surface you are mounting the tether to. If you are mounting to a helmet, there should be a flat enough spot to adhere the small tether mount. Make sure it does not block the view of the shot when your camera is mounted.

• Follow these **steps to attach the tether to your camera**:

1. Remove the backdoor from the Frame.
2. Insert the end of the tether string around the bar on the bottom of the backdoor.
3. Insert the end of the tether string through itself to form a loop.
4. Reattach the backdoor to the Frame.
5. Before attaching your camera to the mount, insert the end of the tether string through the opening on the tether mount.
6. Pull the string through and loop it over the camera.
7. Pull the string tight just under the camera so you have formed a loop that holds tight onto your camera.

OTHER AVAILABLE VERSIONS:

• You can also make a chain of clear zip ties to connect your camera to a stable object. Attach one end of the chain to the object and the other end to your camera. Make sure the diameter of the zip tie connected to your mount is small enough that the camera or mount can't slip through it.

HELMET & WEARABLE MOUNTS

Helmet and wearable mounts provide **the ultimate point of view perspective**. These mounts put the camera right next to you for an intimate first person view. There are several ways to mount your HERO7 in a wearable position and each has its time and place. How and where you mount your camera while wearing it has a huge impact on whether you capture captivating footage or something that will just make you dizzy.

TIPS FOR HELMET & WEARABLE MOUNTS

Follow these tips when setting up your camera with a helmet or a wearable mount:

• When your camera is mounted in a location where you can't see your camera's Touch Screen, use the **GoPro App for a live viewfinder** to set up your angle. This will help you to make minor adjustments to get the angle you want. The Touch Screen on your camera is not very helpful when setting up Helmet and Wearable Mounts because you often can't see the back of the camera to adjust the angle.

• For the most interesting footage, **set up your angle with an object in the foreground** (your arms, board, vehicle, etc.) to give you a perspective of what is going on.

• **Use the GoPro App while filming** so you know if and when your camera is recording and to see what mode you are in. It's really hard to tell whether you are recording by listening to the beeps and it is inconvenient to pull your camera off to look at the Touch Screen. When using Voice Control, try to use the beeps to determine if your camera is recording. **One beep sounds when recording starts or stops. 3 beeps sound after a file is saved.**

• Check the angle of your camera to **make sure the horizon is level**. It's a lot easier to make minor adjustments before filming than to correct them during editing.

• **Best Settings for Wearable Mounts.** Because wearable mounts usually require Wide Angle shots and your camera is so close to you, the 4:3 Standard Aspect ratio video settings (4k turned off) will give you the widest field of view.

• While filming with your GoPro mounted to your body, the steadier you can stay, the better your footage will be. For wearable mounts, use the Slow Motion video resolution (1440-60) for the option to **play back shaky videos in slow motion which helps steady the shots.**

• **Make sure your helmet fits correctly.** If your helmet is loose, the extra weight of the camera will make your helmet move around on your head.

• **Helmet Mounting Positions.** The 3 best locations for mounting your camera to a helmet are:
1. Directly **on top of your helmet** using a Curved Adhesive Mount or a Vented Helmet Strap for vented helmets.
2. For helmets without a lip on the front, you can adhere a mount **on the front of your helmet** and use the Helmet Front Mount for some unique angles.
3. On the **side of your helmet**, use the Helmet Side Mount as shown in the Helmet Front and Side Mount section.

HELMET FRONT AND SIDE MOUNT

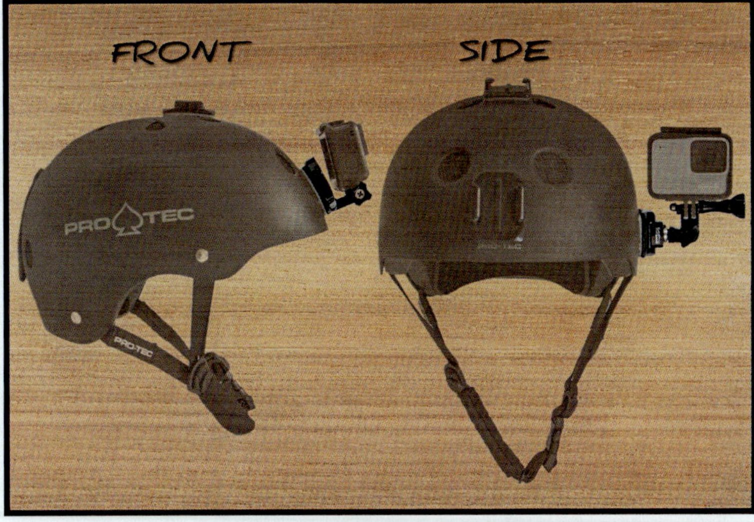

The **Helmet Front Mount** holds your camera onto the front of your helmet and can either point straight forward or point downward for self-portrait shots. The Helmet Front Mount is a great choice for **extreme sports where you want first person point of view footage**. This mount allows for a lower profile angle (as opposed to having the camera on top of your helmet), which means you don't have to compensate for the extra height of the camera above your head. This is especially helpful when going through trees on a bike or snowboarding.

The **Side Mount** is designed for mounting your camera to the side of a helmet for **an eye-level point of view**. With the Side Mount, you can get a portion of your helmet in the foreground for perspective. The Side Mount can also be used to mount your camera to the side of vehicles or any vertical surface. Using these mounts gives you the best possible helmet cam angles.

MOUNTING TIPS:

- Both mounts are used with a Curved Adhesive Mount adhered to your helmet.
- A helmet that has a visor or lip on the front will prevent you from being able to mount this on the very front of your helmet, where it works best. For a helmet with a visor, attach an adhesive mount **directly under the visor** for a similar perspective.
- **For the Front Mount:** Extending your camera out from the front of your helmet pointing down for a self-portrait perspective creates a unique, but very distorted view that makes your head look large and body small. Using an extension to add more distance can help to improve the angle.
- Depending on what type of action you are filming, when the camera is mounted on front of your helmet, **point the camera slightly down** so that you don't just record footage of the sky.
- **For the Side Mount:** One way to use the Side Mount is to mount your camera upright as pictured. You can also flip your camera upside down so the camera angle is closer to your eye level. Your camera will automatically flip the orientation if Landscape Lock is turned Off in the Preferences Menu.
- If you are using **a vented helmet** that doesn't have enough room for a Curved Adhesive Mount, **use the Vented Helmet Strap mount.** The Vented Helmet Strap Mount features two straps designed to be fed through the vents on your **vented helmet** and tightened for a secure temporary mounting position. This is a popular choice for bikers.
- Make sure your helmet fits securely so the extra weight of the camera doesn't move your helmet. The weight of the camera on your helmet is minimal but noticeable, especially when using the Side Mount with a loose helmet.
- For **low-impact activities or sports where you aren't always wearing a helmet**, check out the **Head Strap** (shown below) and QuickClip. With the Head Strap, you can film a similar angle to the Front Mount even when you aren't wearing a helmet. Just throw it on for casual filming or mellow activities. Wear it over a hat or beanie for a more low-pro look. The center strap can be removed when wearing the Head Strap on your head or left on if you are wearing it over a helmet. The Head Strap is not recommended for watersports because if it comes off, it's gone.

MOUNTING EXAMPLE:

MOUNTED ON THE HEAD STRAP FOR A SIMILAR ANGLE

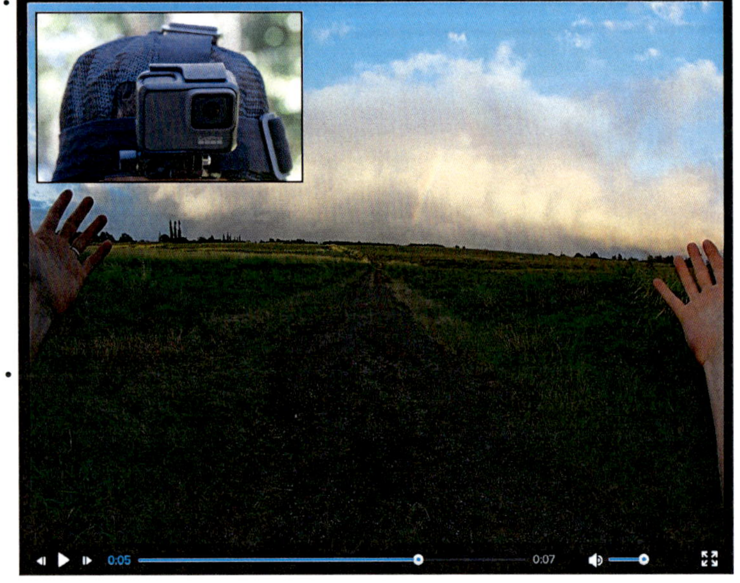

SETTING USED FOR THE ACTION SHOT: Recorded in Video Mode on the HERO7 Silver with Slow Motion turned on (1440 @ 60 FPS WIDE). Slow Motion was selected because it records at a Standard 4:3 Aspect Ratio, which captures the widest perspective possible for this point of view angle. 60 frames per second also opens the possibility to play back the video in slow motion, which helps smooth out most shakiness caused by body movements.

The camera was mounted on the Head Strap and placed over a hat. Because the Head Strap puts the camera near your forehead, it captures an angle similar to the Helmet Front Mount without the need for a helmet. Using the Head Strap creates an immersive point of view angle that leaves the filmer's hands free for any activities. By pointing the camera down slightly, you can record the forward-facing view as well as some of the ground.

CHEST HARNESS (aka CHESTY)

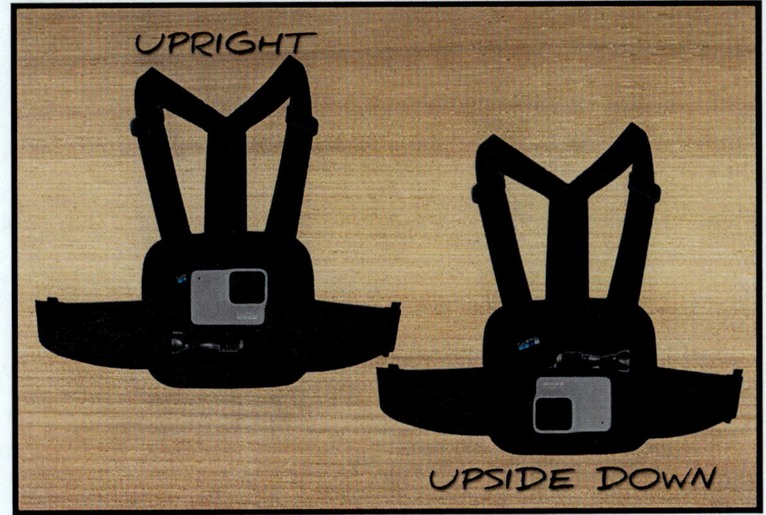

The Chesty (which also comes in a Junior Chesty size for kids 3 years and older) straps over your shoulders and around your body to put your camera right at the middle of your chest. This mount gets your **arms in the shot for a great point of view perspective** for a variety of activities like biking, snowboarding, skiing, motocross, and standup paddling. The Chest Harness puts your camera in position for immersive, smooth point of view shots.

MOUNTING TIPS:

• Mount your camera **upside down for biking or other activities where you are leaning forward** so you can rotate the camera up, pointing it away from the ground.

• Mount your camera **right side up for shots where you are upright** so you can slightly angle your camera down to get some of your body in the frame. You can easily adjust the angle of your camera while it is mounted on your body to see where your camera is pointing.

• The Chest Harness typically can't be used during activities where you lie on your stomach, such as surfing.

MOUNTING EXAMPLES:

MOUNTED ON CHEST WITH CAMERA UPSIDE DOWN

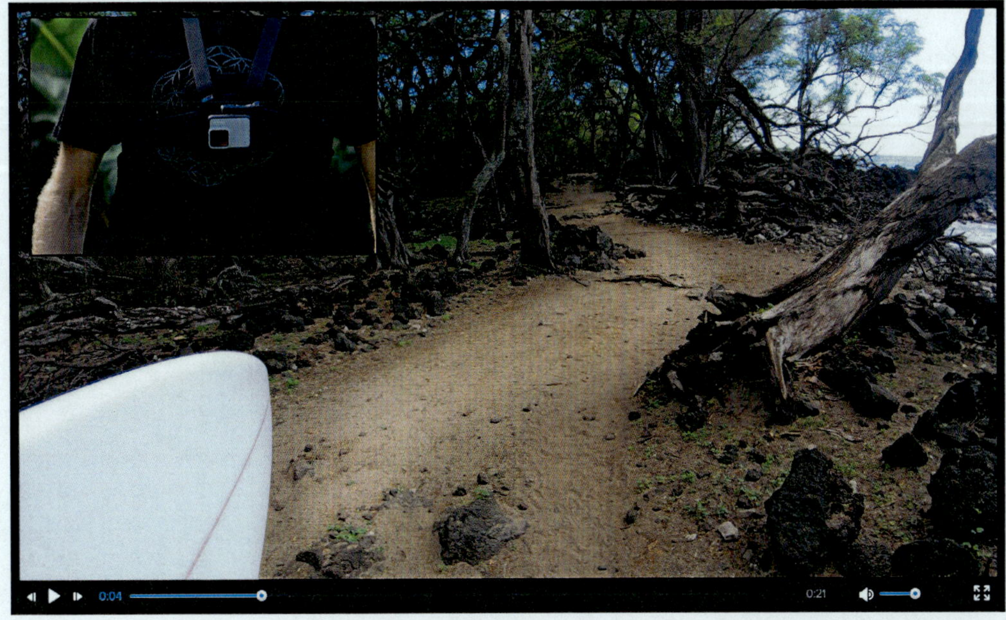

• SETTING USED FOR THE ACTION SHOT: Video recorded on the HERO7 Silver in Video Mode in 4k (4k @ 30 FPS).

• The Frame was mounted upside down to the Vertical Mounting Buckle so it could be tilted up to capture the forward-facing angle.

MOUNTED ON CHEST WITH CAMERA RIGHT SIDE UP

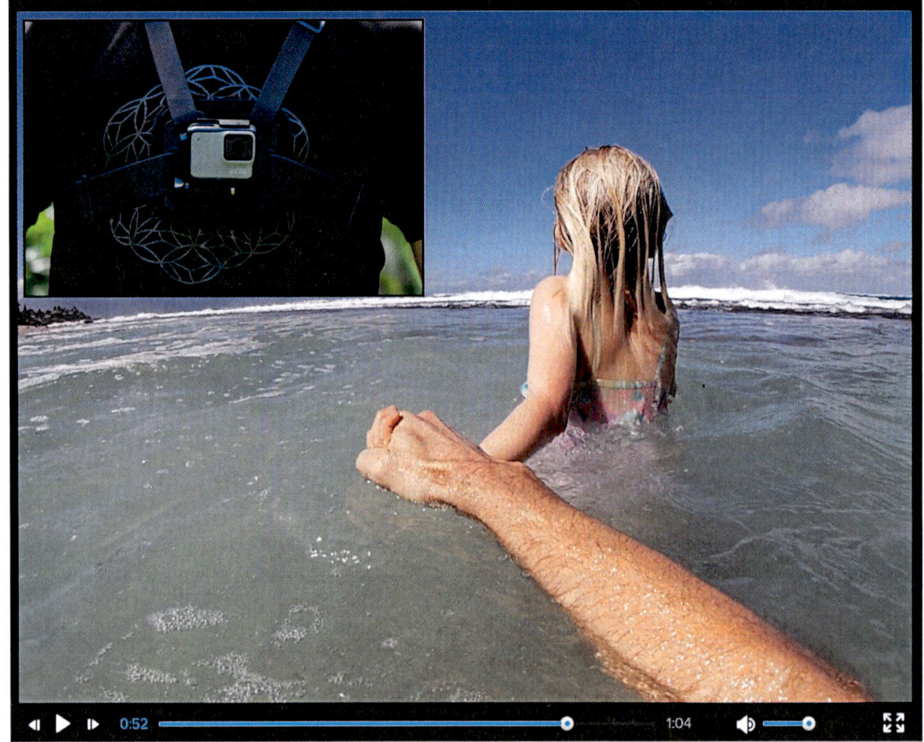

• SETTING USED FOR THE ACTION SHOT: Video recorded on the HERO7 White in Video Mode in Slow Motion (1440 @ 60 FPS). This video setting was selected for the ability to play back the video in slow motion. The Standard 4:3 Aspect Ratio works well for chest mounted shots when the subject is close to the camera. The Slow Motion setting can be selected for nearly all of your video shots unless you want to use Touch Zoom, reduce the frame rate for low light scenes, or on the Silver, record in 4k.

• The Frame was mounted on the Vertical Mounting Buckle to the Chesty so the camera could be angled straight forward or down slightly.

HAND + WRIST STRAP

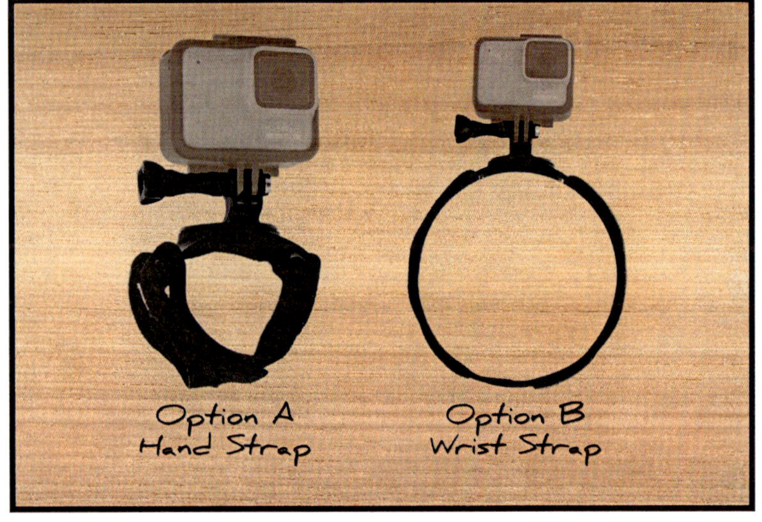

The Hand + Wrist Strap is a **very versatile wearable mount** because it comes with two straps **to fit different diameter objects**. The Strap can be worn around your hand, wrist, ankle, or other round objects (such as a tree branch, bike frame or pole) for unique angles that are difficult to capture with other mounts. The mounting piece rotates 360 degrees allowing you to adjust your camera and change your angle while your camera is mounted.

MOUNTING TIPS:

• **Use the "Slow Motion" setting** when using this mount for videos with a lot of movement so you can slow down the action. Because your camera is mounted on your limbs, which tend to move a lot, slow motion helps to smooth the shaky shots.

• **Reattaching the straps can be confusing** if you forget how they were attached. When changing straps, each end of the tabs is inserted into the mounting piece and folded back onto itself so the GoPro logo is showing.

• When wearing a backpack, tighten the hand strap **around one of the backpack straps** for a forward-facing view.

MOUNTING EXAMPLE:

MOUNTED ON HAND

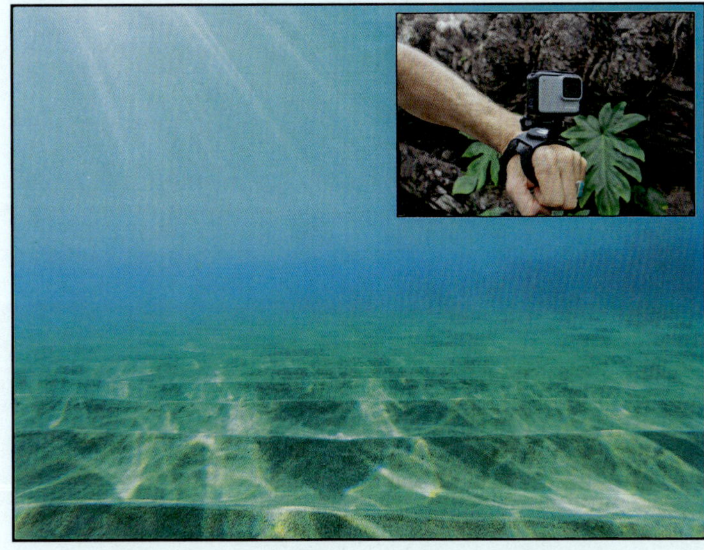

• SETTING USED FOR THE ACTION SHOT: Photo taken on the HERO7 Silver in Photo Mode. The Strap was used for an easy hands-free way to carry the camera and take photos or switch over to Video Mode when something interesting happened.

• During the dive, the HERO7 was rotated on the Hand Strap mount to create a variety of angles depending on the scene but was mostly pointed forward to take photos of underwater scenes and sea creatures.

VERSATILE MOUNTS

The mounts in this section **can be used in a variety of ways to capture unique angles**. These mounts are grouped together because they **can be mounted temporarily to a variety of objects**. Each of these mounts is quite unique and specific usage tips are given at each mount.

HANDLE OR POLECAM/MONOPOD

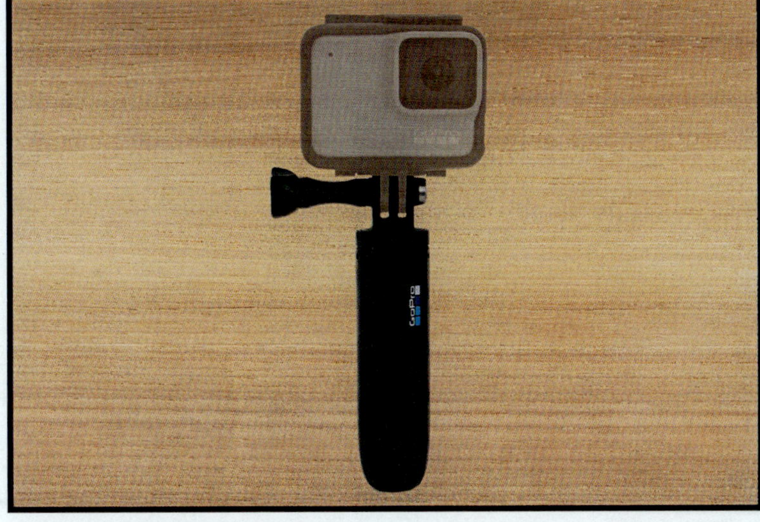

Attach your HERO7 to a handle (typically about 6"-8") or a pole (18"+) for an easy way to hold your camera and **capture multiple angles with one mount**. A handle or pole (also known as a selfie stick) enables you to capture some of the best angles possible for any activity where you have a free hand. The pole creates distance between you and your camera to include more of the scene in handheld self-portraits. You can **film yourself, follow behind your friends, or hold the pole vertically** to get more height on your shots.

There are tons of options available for a well-designed handle or pole, or you can easily make your own (see the Handlebar/ Seatpost Mounting tips for simple instructions).

If you are looking to purchase a premade handle, check out the Handler (by GoPro), or the Bobber (by GoPole). Both options are waterproof and will float your camera. The GoPro Shorty (pictured above) is a compact option that doubles as a mini tripod.

For a well-designed pole, the 3-Way by GoPro is very versatile and can capture multiple angles when used with the extension arm extended. GoPro also makes El Grande, which is an extension pole that can reach from 15" up to 38" for a more heavy duty selfie stick. GoScope also makes a telescoping pole and GoPole makes the Evo, which is clear, floats and is extendable from 14"-24". A cheap lightweight option is the Bower Xtreme Action Monopod.

MOUNTING TIPS:

• **Hold the pole as steady as possible** while filming for smooth shots.

• See the examples for the **three primary ways to hold your camera** when using a handle or polecam.

MOUNTING EXAMPLES:

THE FOLLOW-ALONG ANGLE

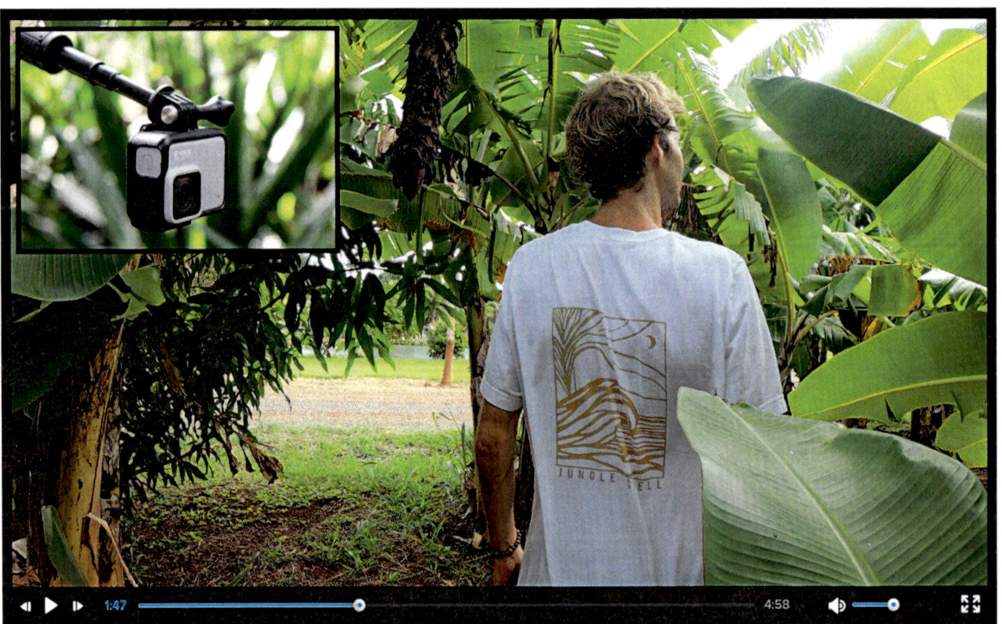

• Because the camera is upside down and facing out, the weight of the camera naturally helps to stabilize your shots, providing **optimal stability for following behind your friends both in and out of the water**.

• SETTING USED FOR THE ACTION SHOT: Video recorded on the HERO7 Silver in Video Mode in 4k (4k @ 30 FPS). The lower frame rate of 30 FPS worked well to compensate for the low light of this shaded scene filmed on a slightly overcast day.

• The Frame was mounted on the GoPro Shorty with the pole extended and held upside down as shown in the example for stability.

• When your camera is mounted upside down like this, set Landscape Lock to Down so you can preview your footage right side up or turn it off to allow auto-rotation.

UPRIGHT POLECAM

• The upright mounting position gives you **extra height to take photos or videos,** usually of other people or subjects. When using a long pole, it can be hard to reach your camera to press the Shutter Button. Recording videos is easy because you can start recording before the action begins. But for Photo and Burst modes,, use the Self-Timer or use Voice Control to remotely press the Shutter.

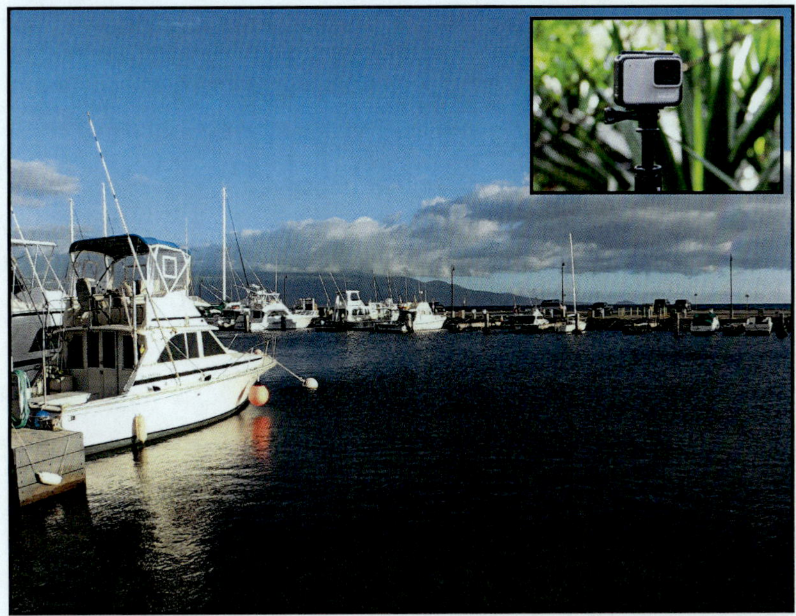

• SETTING USED FOR THE ACTION SHOT: Photo taken with the HERO7 White in Photo Mode. Touch Zoom was used to zoom in on the scene to reduce the wide angle effect.

• The camera was mounted on the GoPro Shorty and held as shown in the example photo. The upright angle allows easy access to view and compose your shots using the Touch Screen.

SELFIE SHOT

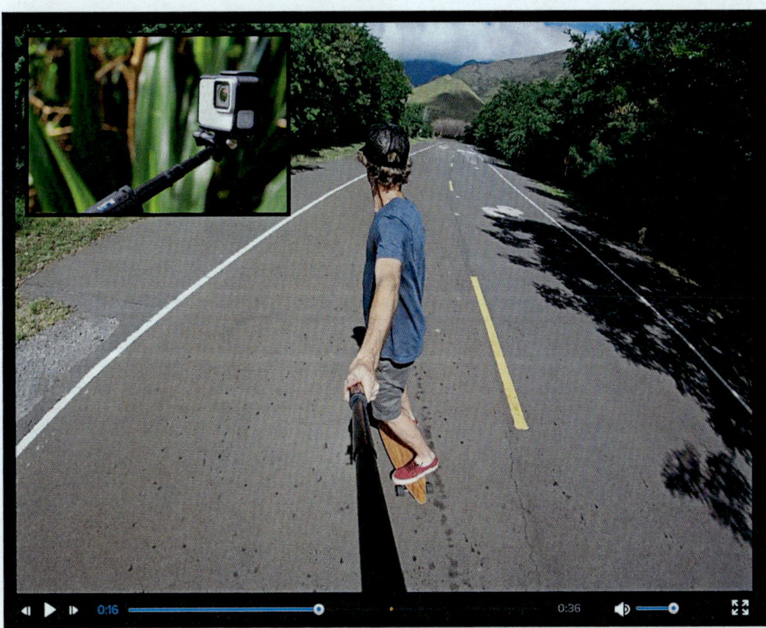

• When you have a free hand to hold the handle or pole, this mounting position creates distance between you and your camera for a better selfie point of view shot. Angle the camera up and away from the pole slightly as shown to capture less of the pole and more of you in the shot.

• SETTING USED FOR THE ACTION SHOT: Video recorded on the HERO7 Silver in Video Mode in Slow Motion (1440 @ 60 FPS). 1440p works well for selfie shots because of the wide field of view which can be cropped to widescreen 1080p. The bright daylight provided plenty of light to record at 60 FPS for slow motion.

• The Frame was mounted to GoPro's El Grande pole using the Vertical Mounting Buckle for maximum rotation. The long extension of El Grande allowed for a more pulled back selfie shot to capture more of the surrounding scene.

HANDLEBAR / SEATPOST POLE MOUNT (pictured) & LARGE TUBE MOUNT

       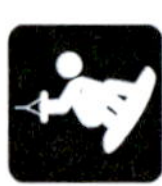 

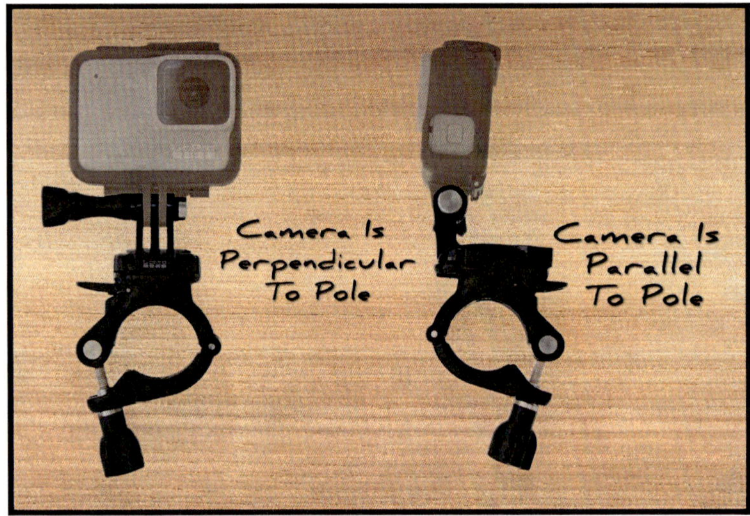

The Large Tube Mount and the Handlebar/Seatpost Pole Mount are very similar. Both mounts consist of a round mounting piece that **clamps together around a pole** and tightens using a single bolt. The mounting buckle on top can be rotated 360 degrees with 16 locking positions to adjust your camera for the perfect angle. GoPro also makes a Pro Handlebar/Seatpost Pole Mount made of aluminum for extra strength, specifically for biking.

The Handlebar Seatpost Mount fits poles and tubes that are .75" to 1.40" (1.90cm - 3.50cm) in diameter. The Large Tube Mount fits onto larger pipes and poles with a diameter from 1.40" to 2.50" (3.50cm-6.35cm).

These two mounts are very versatile, although the Handlebar Seatpost Mount fits on a wider variety of objects.

Some ways you can use **the Handlebar/Seatpost Mount** are:
• Mount it on a piece of PVC pipe or a long stick for **an easy homemade polecam**.
• Mount it **to a paddle** while riding waves standup paddling.
• Put it **on ski poles** or on the ski rack in a sled.
• Mount it **to the roof racks** of a car or truck for Time Lapse videos of your adventures.
• Attach your camera on **bike handlebars, a seatpost or a bike frame** (depending on the bike).

Use **the Roll Bar Mount** to:
• Mount your camera to the **strut of an airplane**.
• Attach it **to a bike frame** (for larger diameter frames).

MOUNTING TIPS:

• When **mounting the Handlebar Seatpost Mount to your bike**, if your bike seatpost is long enough, mount the Handlebar Seatpost Mount low on the seatpost with the camera mounted upright so that your legs don't rub on it while riding.

• Tighten the thumbscrew that connects your camera with the GoPro Tool or a screwdriver so your camera doesn't change position on bumpy roads or when hit by a wave.

• **Make your own polecam/handle** by attaching the Handlebar/Seatpost Mount to the end of a 3/4" diameter piece of PVC pipe. Spray paint the PVC pipe with a matte black paint so it looks more stealth in your shots. If you are using the pole in the water, seal both ends with waterproof epoxy (Waterweld Epoxy works well) so it floats. Slide a rubber bike handlebar grip on the end if you want the extra grip. See the previous mounting section (Handle and Polecam) for more tips on how to use a polecam.

• When mounting to painted metal or other slippery surfaces, put the included protective liner around the pole to **prevent the mount from slipping**. The rubber also reduces vibration during filming.

• The Vertical Mounting Buckle gives you a wider range of motion to adjust your camera's angle, while the Mounting Buckle creates a more low-profile setup.

MOUNTING EXAMPLE:

MOUNTED TO PADDLE (CAMERA PERPENDICULAR TO POLE)

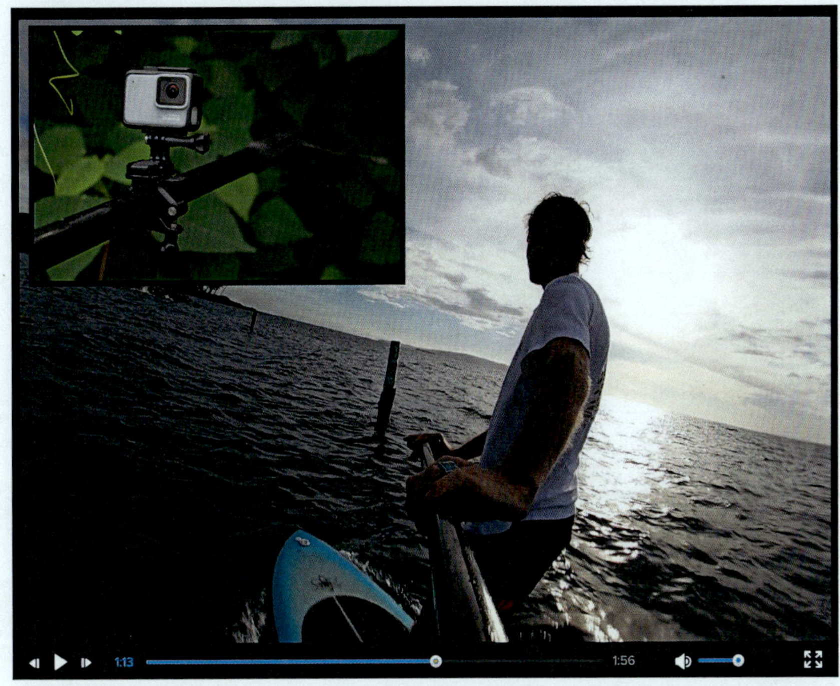

- SETTING USED FOR THE ACTION SHOT: Video recorded on the HERO7 Silver in Video Mode in Slow Motion (1440 @ 60 FPS). 1440p was chosen to capture as much of the scene as possible since the camera was mounted relatively close to the subject.
- The Handlebar Seatpost Mount is mounted near the base of a paddle. The mount can be rotated to capture the angle you want.
- When mounted to a stick or pole like shown, tilt your camera back to capture less of the pole in the foreground and more of the scene.

SUCTION CUP MOUNT

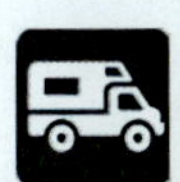 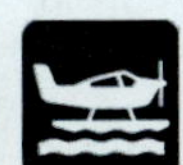   

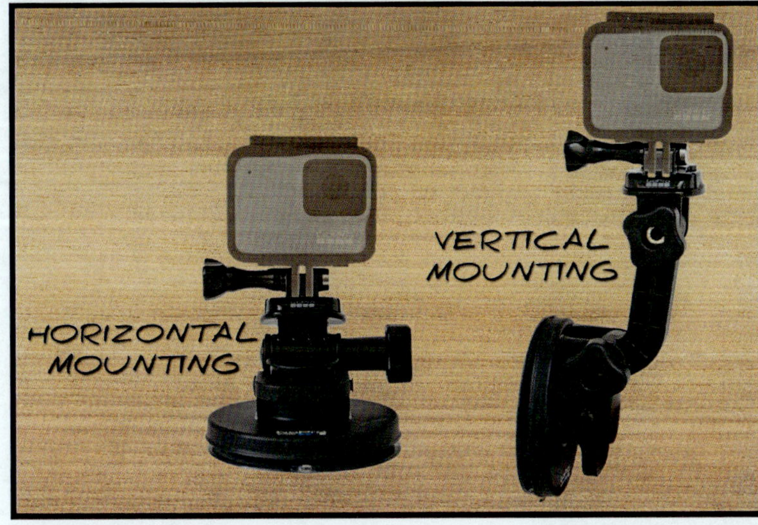

A suction cup mount uses an industrial strength suction cup at the base of the mount to **temporarily mount your GoPro camera** to a variety of surfaces including cars, trucks, boats and some sporting equipment. It comes with adjustable arms so you can customize the camera orientation for the shot you want.

The Suction Cup Mount is **the perfect travel mount** because you can temporarily mount your GoPro camera without using an adhesive mount. This mount also gives you the freedom to **quickly move your camera** to capture several angles.

MOUNTING TIPS:

- Make sure you **attach the Suction Cup Mount to a flat, clean and smooth surface**, such as glass or smooth metal. Check to see that the suction cup is clear of debris. The suction cup will not stick well to a porous, curved or flexible surface.
- The Suction Cup Mount is **NOT recommended for high-impact sports** like snowboarding, motocross, or surfing.
- Do NOT apply the Suction Cup Mount in an environment where the temperature is drastically different than where you will be using the Suction Cup Mount. If you are in the snow for example, don't attach the Suction Cup Mount in your heated car and then jump outside into the cold. This may affect the suction.

• **Wet the edge of the ring** with a little bit of saliva or water before pushing the suction cup onto the surface to get better suction.

• After pushing down the button and flipping over the lever to secure the mount, **pull firmly on the mount to test its suction**. When mounted correctly, the mount should not move at all.

• If you are using this mount in a situation where you will lose your camera if the mount comes off, **use a leash tether or lanyard attached to a separate Tether Mount** as backup in case the suction cup does fail. You can also use a chain of zip ties attached to a part of your vehicle if you don't want to apply an adhesive tether. Attach the other end of the zip tie chain to the arm of the Suction Cup Mount. You don't want to lose your camera!

• Use the Suction Cup Mount in the water cautiously. If you are using a Suction Cup Mount in water, be sure to use a Floaty to provide flotation for your camera. And use a tether mount when possible just in case the Suction Cup fails.

MOUNTING EXAMPLE:

MOUNTED TO THE SIDE OF A VEHICLE

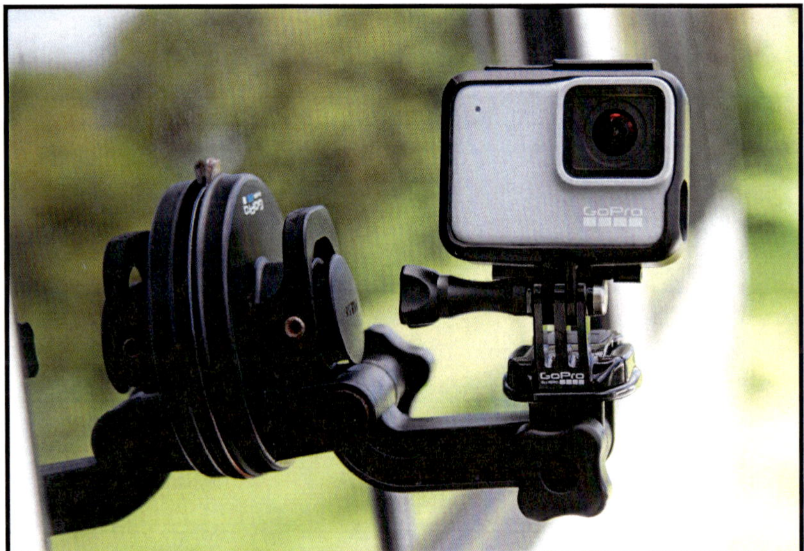

• The camera shown here is mounted outside of a car window. The window was wiped clean first and the suction cup was pulled hard to test its suction before driving.

FOR WINDSHIELD/WINDOW MOUNTING

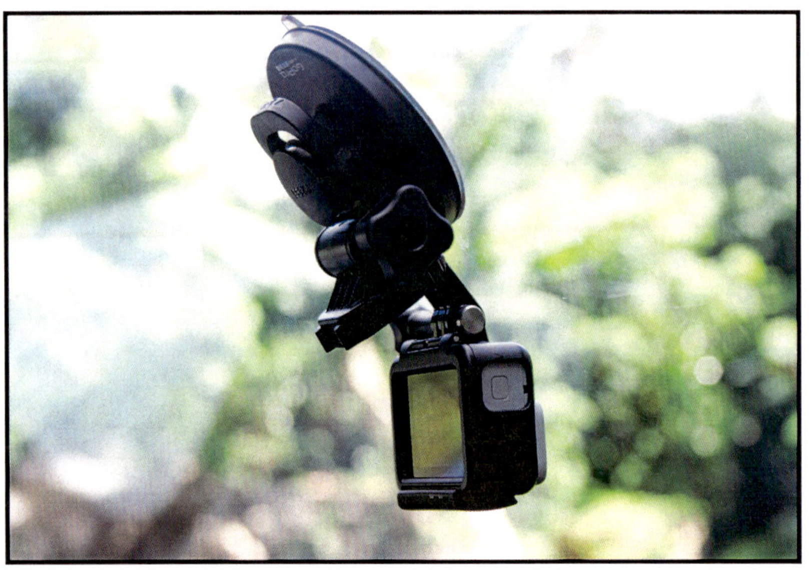

• When mounting your camera to a car windshield or airplane window, mount your camera upside down to get as close to the glass as possible, which will reduce reflections.

• The Frame was mounted to the Vertical Mounting Buckle for more clearance past the bottom edge of the Suction Cup Mount.

OTHER AVAILABLE VERSIONS:

• The RAM Suction Cup Mount for GoPro has ball joints on the end for easy adjusting.

TRIPOD MOUNT

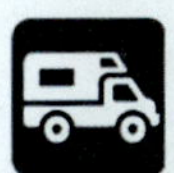    

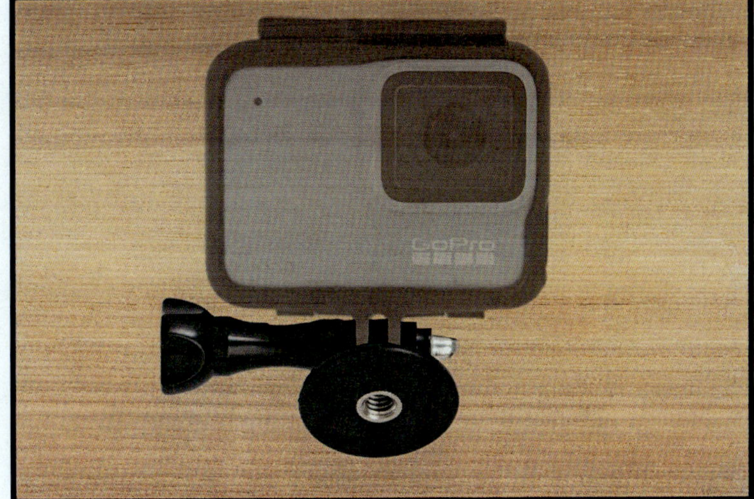

The Tripod Mount is a small mount that has a standard 1/4"-20 threads per inch screw so you can **mount your camera to any tripod**. This mount, as small and simple as it is, really opens up a lot of possibilities for different shots to mix in with your other action shots, such as scenic shots and self-portraits where you set up the shot and then pass by the camera.

MOUNTING TIPS:

• A tripod is the best partner to utilize this mount. The mount comes with a basic tripod. A small, flexible tripod like the inexpensive Dynex Flexible Tripod or the Joby GorillaPod opens up a myriad of options for unique angles.

• The Tripod Mount also comes with a Quick Release Tripod Mount allowing you to easily slide your camera on and off of a tripod.

• Because this mount enables you to attach your camera to any 1/4"-20 screw, there are tons of custom mounting options, including on top of a DSLR or mirrorless camera to record video in addition to the photos you take with your DSLR. (See ON TOP OF A DSLR Example for mounting instructions.)

MOUNTING EXAMPLES:

ON A TRIPOD

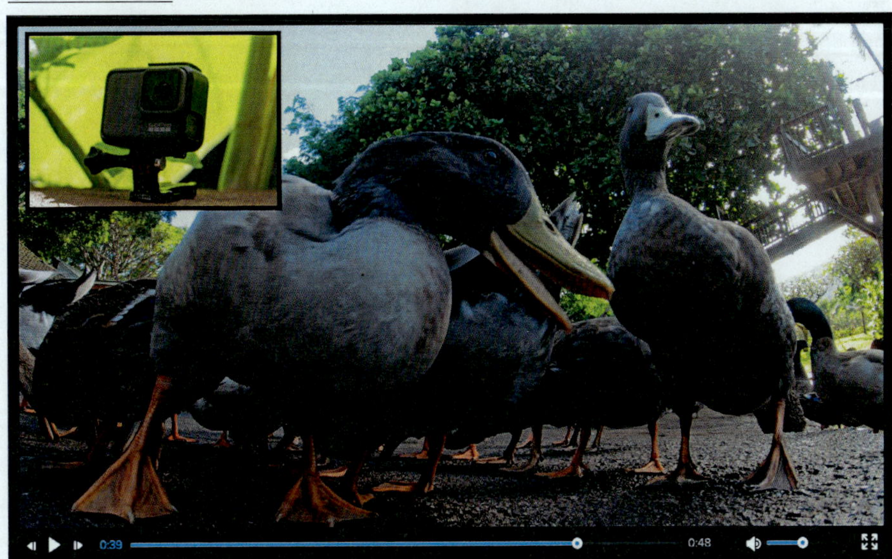

• SETTING USED FOR THE ACTION SHOT: Video recorded on the HERO7 Silver in Video Mode in 4k (4k @ 30 FPS). No slow motion was needed since this was a stationary shot.

• Use the Tripod Mount or the Quick Release Tripod Mount to mount your HERO7 on any mini or full-size tripod. For a full-size tripod, a fluid-head is the best option for smooth video movements.

• This example shows that sometimes you can also make do with what you have. The camera was propped up on the ground using only the Mounting Buckle and Frame to mimic a tripod shot. By being creative with what you have, you can mimic some of these mounted shots even when you don't have all of your mounts with you.

ON TOP OF A MIRRORLESS CAMERA

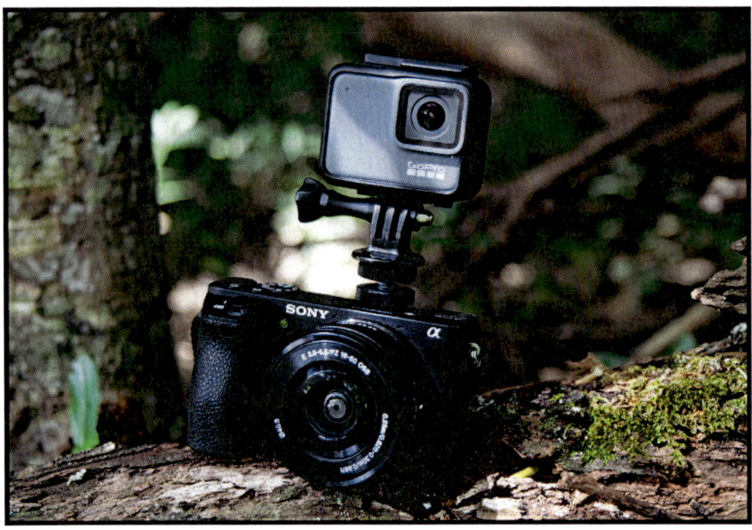

• Use a Hot Shoe to 1/4"-20 Tripod Screw Adapter (available online, but not from GoPro) along with the Tripod Mount to mount your HERO7 to the top of your DSLR or mirrorless camera so you can record video or Time Lapse videos with your GoPro while taking photos with your DSLR.

• If you are shooting with a standard lens on your DSLR, the lens will most likely be out of the GoPro video frame. However, check the shot on the Touch Screen If the lens is in your shot, rotate your HERO7 up to get the lens out of the frame or zoom in for a tighter shot.

JAWS: FLEX CLAMP

   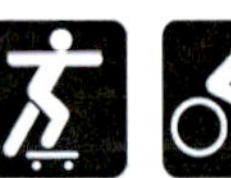 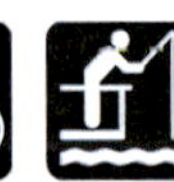 

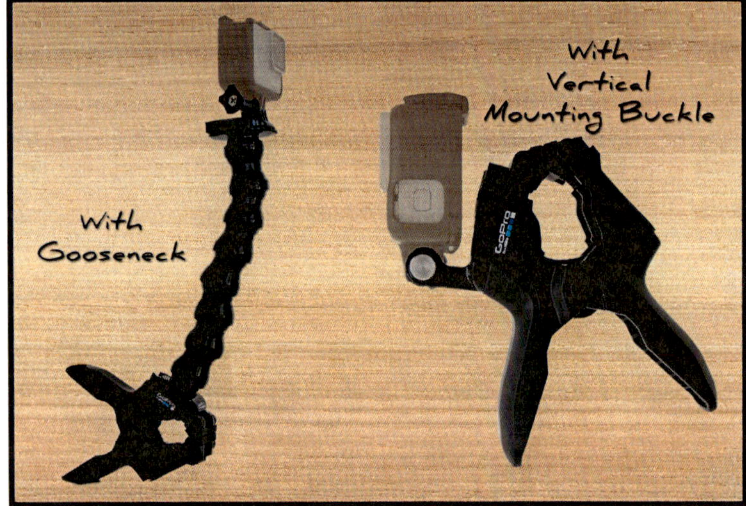

The Jaws: Flex Clamp has a **very strong grip** and comes with a flexible arm that can be used for a variety of mounting options. The clamp can be quickly and easily mounted and removed for **easy shots on the go**.

MOUNTING TIPS:

• Use a **Vertical Mounting Buckle in conjunction with the clamp** so you can rotate your camera all the way back when needed for the correct angle.

• The Gooseneck Extension gives you **flexibility to reposition your camera** into multiple angles from one clamping location.

• The **rubber tab** on the clamp can be **pulled to tighten the grip** when you are clamped onto a round object.

• Jaws **can also be used as a handle**. Hold the clamp in your hands with the camera upside down facing out for maximum stability.

• The Jam (Adjustable Music Mount) by GoPro is another clamp-style mount designed for mounting to musical instruments. The clamp is more lightweight for a lighter option.

MOUNTING EXAMPLES:

WITH THE GOOSENECK ON AN UKULELE

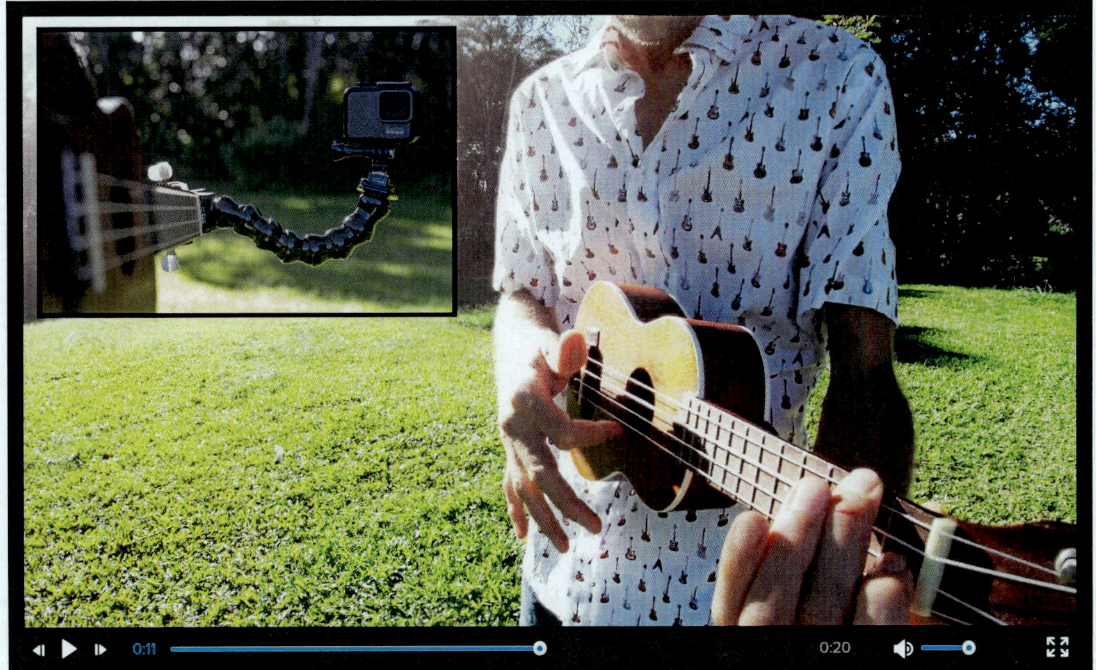

• SETTING USED FOR THE ACTION SHOT: Video recorded on the HERO7 Silver in Video Mode in 4k (4k @ 30 FPS) for the highest quality video possible on this camera.

• The Frame was mounted to the Swivel Buckle on the Gooseneck for the widest range of motion to capture this unique angle.

OTHER AVAILABLE VERSIONS:

(Both of the following options require the Tripod Mount to mount your GoPro to their products)

• ActionPod offers the Action Clamp, which is a clamp with a bendy arm.

• Pedco also makes a wide variety of camera clamps.

CHEAP & EASY DO-IT-YOURSELF GOPRO MOUNTS

GoPro'ers are a creative bunch who have taken underground no-frills filmmaking to the next level. Custom mounts are one of the easiest ways to capture unique shots. The key is to keep them cheap or else you might as well go buy a professionally-made version. These cheap and easy custom mount ideas will give you a head start on your image-making.

BACKPACK POLECAM (THIRD PERSON MOUNT)

The Backpack Pole Mount creates one of the coolest angles around. Also called the Third Person Mount, this custom mount **captures a perspective of your camera following you from behind**. This mount is NOT MADE for HIGH-IMPACT activities and is not waterproof, but for leisurely activities, this mount is perfect to get a full angle of the action with you in center stage. The mount is framed into your backpack so it creates a steady shot of you as the scenery moves around you.

To make this mount, use three pieces of PVC pipe and four 90º PVC Elbows to build a frame that fits around the bottom and sides of your backpack. Then join the top of the PVC pipe together using two short pieces of PVC pipe with a PVC Tee in the middle. Add another PVC pole into the tee with the Handlebar Seatpost mount on the end to mount your camera and you are ready to go film.

CABLE SLIDER

A cable slider allows you to slide your camera along a cable for a smooth movement through the air. If you are using a drone, you wouldn't really need to make one of these because this shot resembles a drone shot. But, for those of you who don't have a drone, there are some relatively easy DIY versions online for making your own cable slider.

To use a cable slider, you will need the right filming location with two high objects for connecting the cable. These shots look great with your camera traveling through the trees along a path.

EGG TIMER TIME LAPSE

The Ikea Ordning Egg Timer costs about $6 and works great for a rotating camera mount to shoot time lapses or hyperlapses. You can stick a mount directly on top of the timer, choose your time lapse settings based on the shot and the egg timer will slowly move counterclockwise. You can't adjust the rotating speed of the timer (360 degrees in one hour), which is far too slow for regular speed video, but for $6 US, this is a great way to add some movement to your time lapse clips.

FOLLOW YOUR PASSION

The following diagrams illustrate some of the best mounts and mounting locations for some of the most popular adventure sports. Of course, there are more sports and activities for your adventurous lifestyle, but **these are a starting point to inspire you to get out there and start filming with your HERO7.** As you figure out which angles and locations work well for you, your ideas and knowledge will expand and even more ideas for creative mounting locations will come to mind.

As far as settings, use the Slow Motion video setting for all of these mounting locations, unless you want to record in 4k with the HERO7 Silver.

WATER SPORTS

Use a Floaty Backdoor (when the mounts allow it) or a floating handle for all watersports. Also, since the touch functions won't work properly with wet hands, lock the Touch Screen and use the alternative button method to change settings.

SNORKELING / DIVING

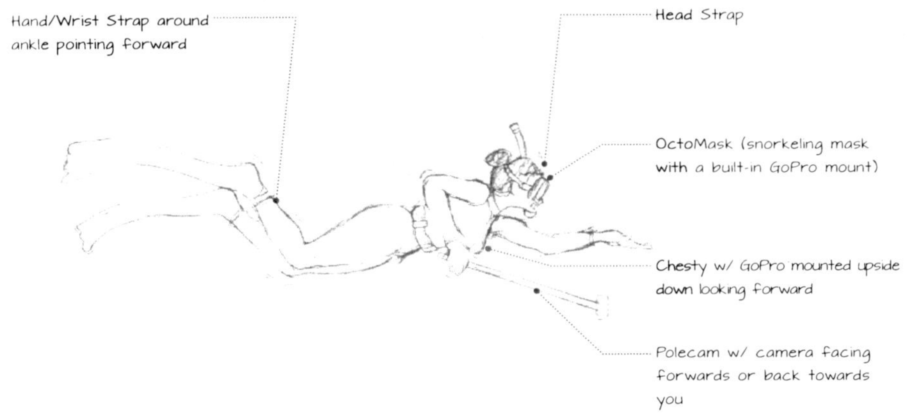

Hand/Wrist Strap around ankle pointing forward

Head Strap

OctoMask (snorkeling mask with a built-in GoPro mount)

Chesty w/ GoPro mounted upside down looking forward

Polecam w/ camera facing forwards or back towards you

SURFING

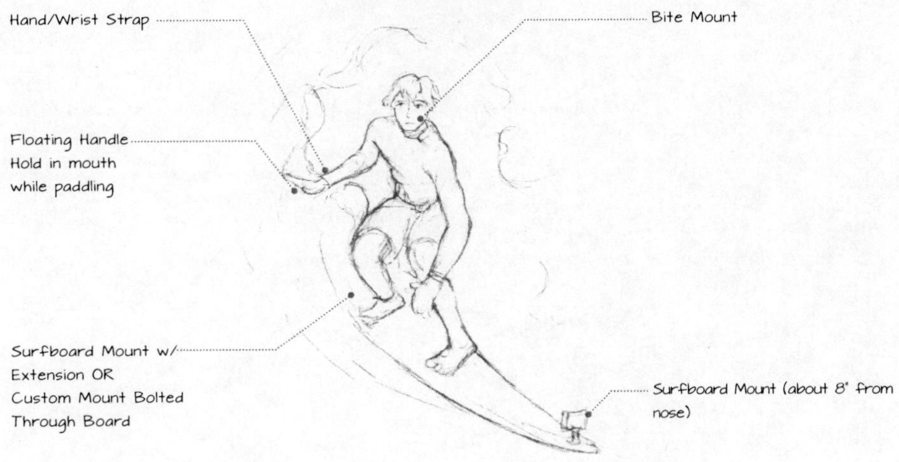

STAND UP PADDLING

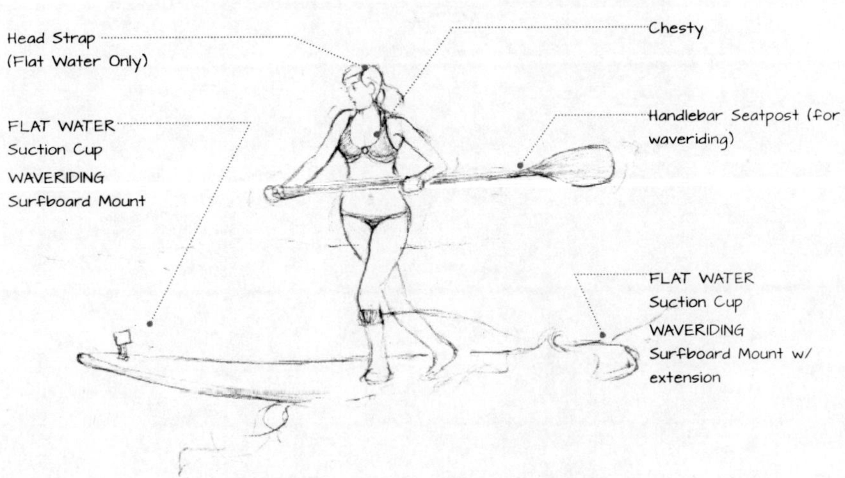

KAYAKING

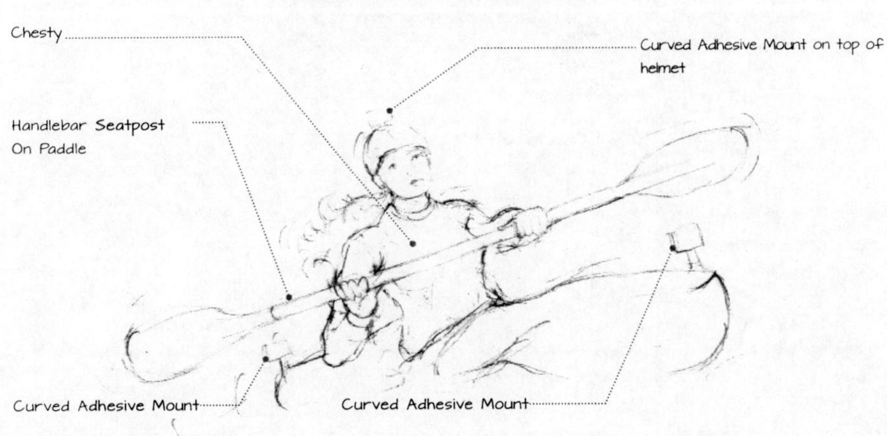

KITE/WAKEBOARDING

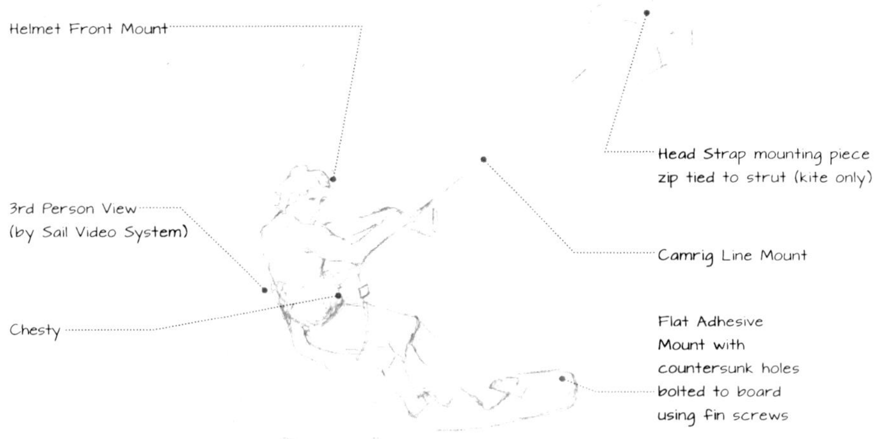

LAND SPORTS

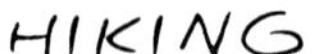

HIKING

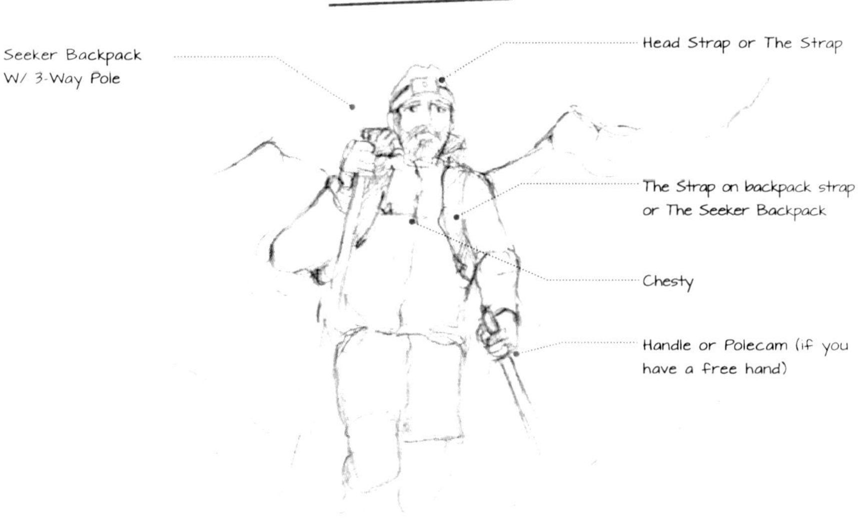

BIKING & MOTORCYCLE

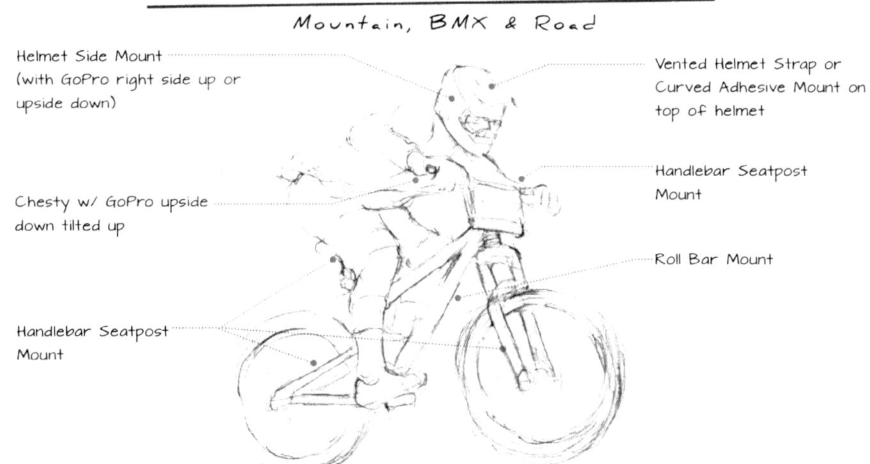

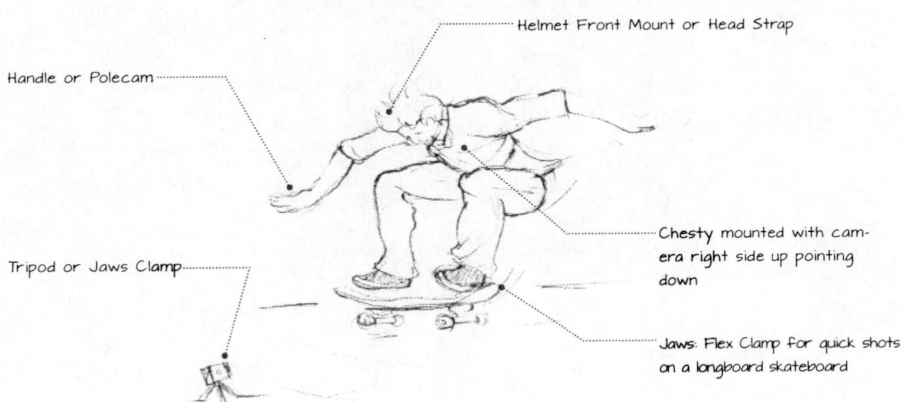

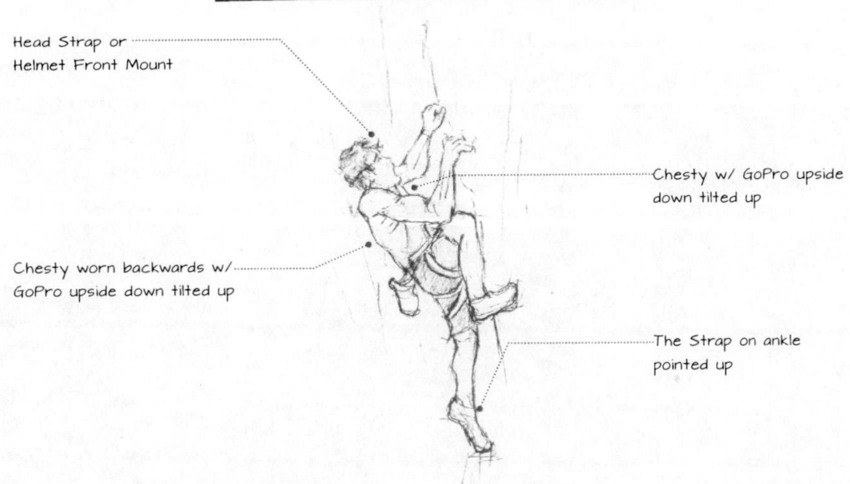

SKATEBOARDING
Helmet Front Mount or Head Strap
Handle or Polecam
Chesty mounted with camera right side up pointing down
Tripod or Jaws Clamp
Jaws: Flex Clamp for quick shots on a longboard skateboard

ROCK CLIMBING
Head Strap or Helmet Front Mount
Chesty w/ GoPro upside down tilted up
Chesty worn backwards w/ GoPro upside down tilted up
The Strap on ankle pointed up

SKIING
Curved Adhesive Mount on top of helmet
Handlebar Seatpost Mount on ski pole. Hold in front or behind you for selfie.
Helmet Front Mount OR Head Strap over helmet
The Strap around boot
Chesty (with camera right side up)

SNOW SPORTS

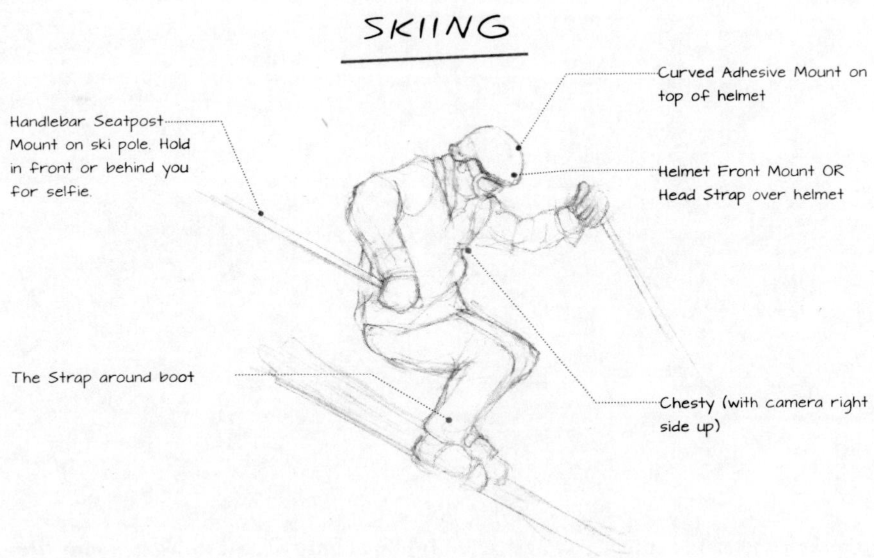

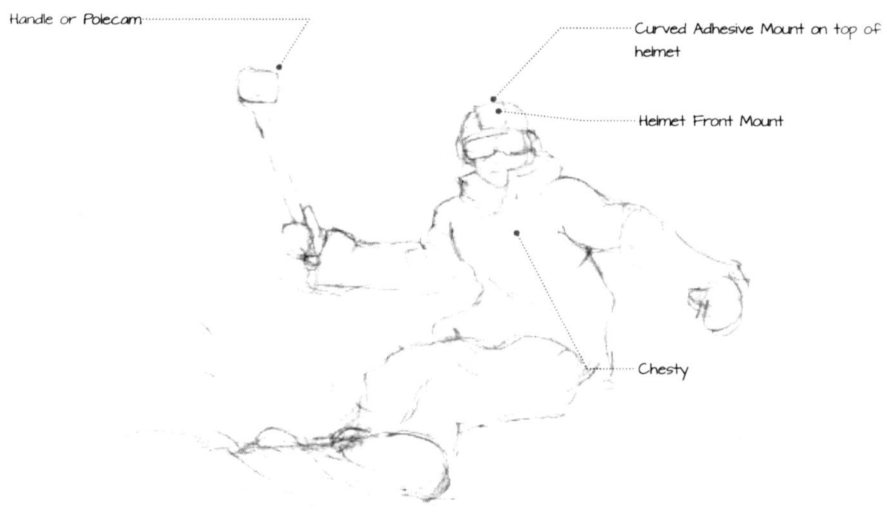

AIR SPORTS

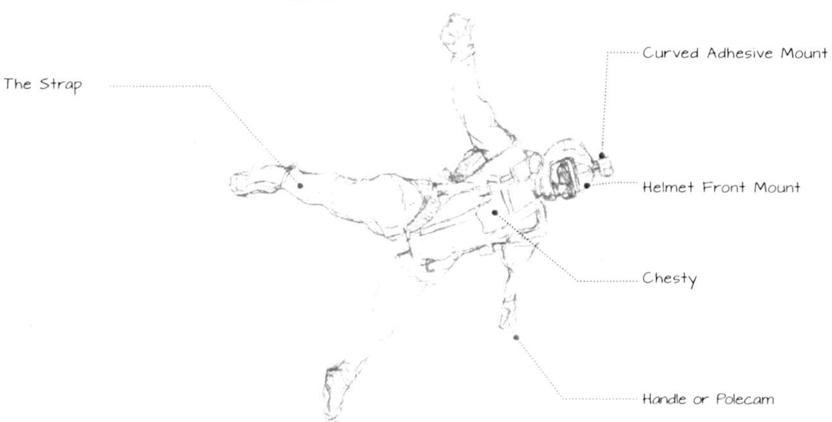

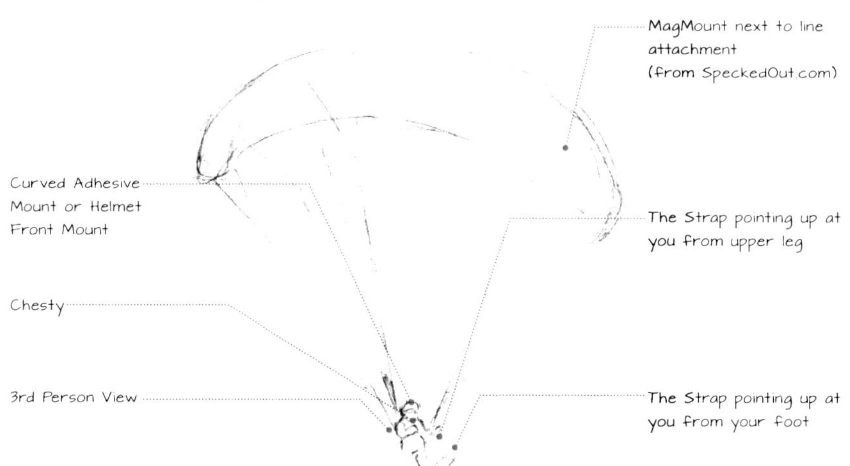

Now that you've got your camera mounted, you are ready to move onto Step 4 to learn some vital photography and cinematography knowledge!

STEP FOUR

CAPTURE YOUR ACTION

Learn These "Not-So-Secret" Photography Secrets & Get Results

Now that your camera is set up and ready, it's time to hit that record button. Whether you are shooting video or photos, there are a few important elements that are (almost) always part of a memorable photograph or video. The shooting tips in this step will help you capture the footage you know your HERO7 is capable of- the kind of immersive, exciting videos and photos that motivated you to get your camera in the first place.

TELL A STORY

When planning shots for your video, remember that you want to tell a story. If you want to make a video that grabs your viewers' attention, **start thinking about your video before you are out there in the action**. The best GoPro videos inspire us and motivate us to go adventure by telling a story, showing the action, and leaving on a high note.

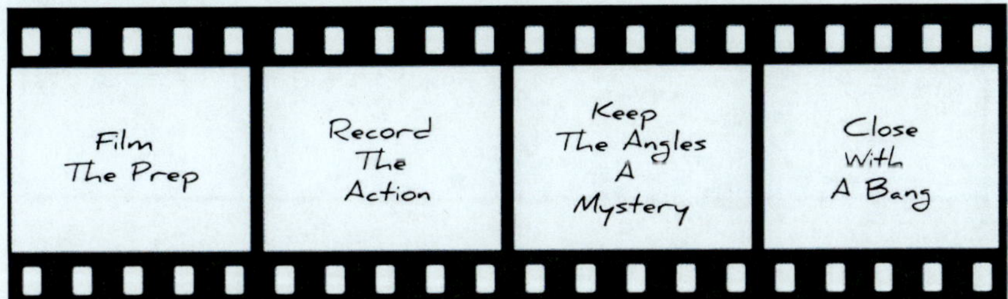

FILM THE PREP

Instead of just recording the main activity, film the preparation. Film a zoomed in close-up when putting on your gear or prepping your important equipment. On your way out, film a pulled back shot leaving for your destination.

RECORD THE ACTION

This is where you can record some or all of the angles shown in this book of the main activity. This is where you show off your skills and most memorable moments with high action shots or beautiful scenery. Record using the slow motion setting so you can slow down the action when you want to.

MAKE THE ANGLES A MYSTERY

When possible, try to **film multiple angles of the same action without seeing any other cameras** in the scene. This keeps the viewer involved in the action, not in the filming techniques. This is where you can apply your newly acquired mounting knowledge.

CLOSE WITH A BANG

Close your video with a dramatic point of view shot that leaves your viewer wanting more, or better yet, wanting to go out there and do what you are doing- having fun!

LIGHTING

In the eyes of most photographers and videographers, lighting is everything. Sometimes the radical action captured with GoPro cameras can overpower less than optimal lighting, but good lighting ALWAYS makes a shot look better.

Figuring out lighting with your mounted camera is especially tricky because you have to foresee how your lighting will be when you are filming. The way you see light in your footage changes dramatically depending on how you mount your camera and the angle you choose to shoot.

When you are preparing for your adventure, think about where the sun will be and what direction you will be facing during the most important times. Then consider what lighting scenario you want for your shot. When using GoPro® cameras, there are so many mounting techniques that there is almost always an angle to capture the lighting you desire.

Wearable mounts offer the least amount of flexibility in regard to where you point your camera. Handheld shots offer the most flexibility because you can adjust your angle to compensate for different lighting scenarios.

Here are some lighting situations you will come across:

THE GOLDEN HOUR (AKA THE MAGIC HOUR IN CINEMATOGRAPHY)

The Golden Hour refers to the hour around sunrise and sunset.

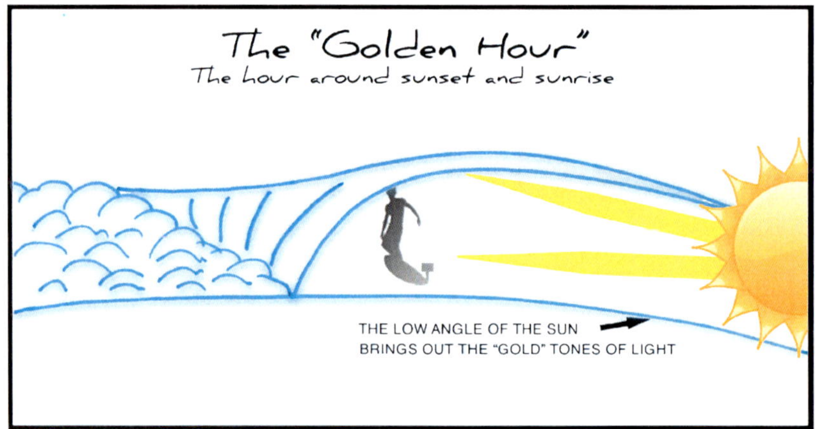

During this time, **lighting is softer and warmer**. Shadows are lighter and longer which can make for a dramatic effect. Sometimes, it can be difficult to keep your own shadow out of the shot during this time, but the results of shooting during these times usually pay off big time. Because the Golden Hour light is not as bright as midday light, follow the recommendations for "Low Light Situations" at the end of this Lighting section.

FRONT LIT LIGHTING

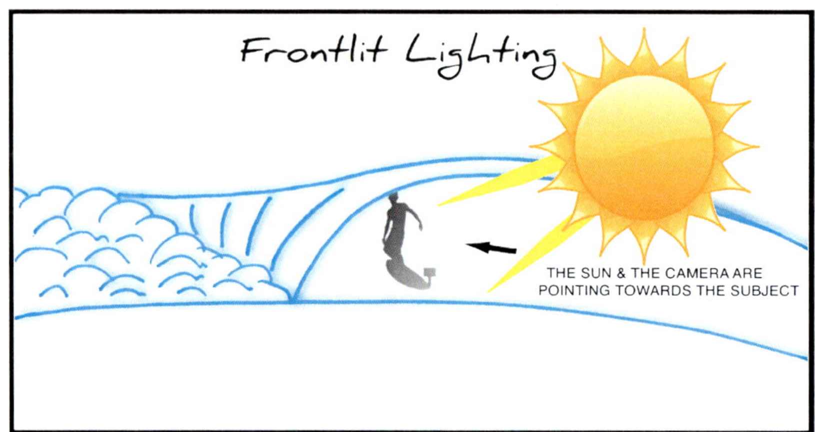

Front lit lighting is when the light from the **sun is on the subject's face** and the camera is between the sun and the subject. The sun and camera are both directed towards the subject. Front-lit lighting tends to result in the bluest skies and best scenic colors, but it also causes harsh shadows on people which can sometimes be less than flattering.

Front lit lighting is the rule that most of us have heard at least once and probably 100 times. "Have the sun behind you when you take a picture!" Front lit is one of the best ways to light a photograph. Depending on the orientation of your scene, front lit lighting can occur either through the morning or the evening hours.

BACKLIT LIGHTING

Backlit lighting is when the **sun is behind the subject**, usually causing the subject to be too dark against a bright background.

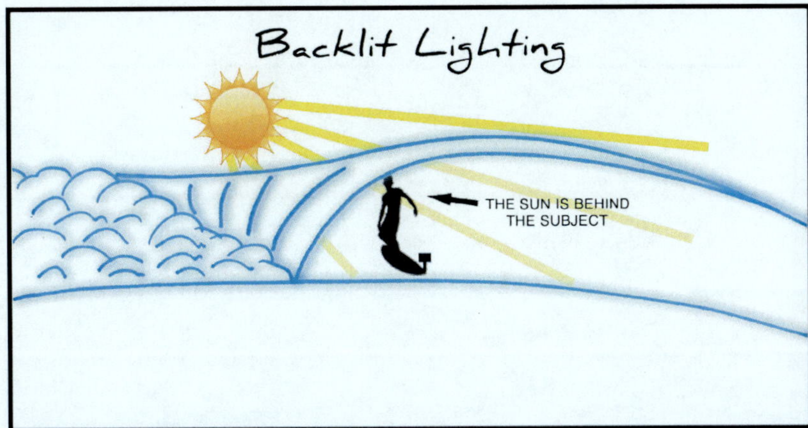

There are positive aspects of backlit lighting though. One is that there are no shadows on a person's face, which means a lot of portraits are taken during backlit conditions. Backlit photos in waves also bring out those green, moody photos where the light is shining through the water. This happens in the tube of the wave, so if you can get yourself in the right spot, the results can be beautiful.

The problem with filming in backlit lighting with a GoPro® camera is that the camera will take a "correct" exposure reading for the overall scene which often makes the subject too dark. To correct the exposure on your subject when backlit, you have to override the camera to overexpose the image (making it brighter than the camera thinks it should be). See the next section on Exposure to learn how you can manually override your camera's exposure reading.

CLOUDY LIGHTING

Cloudy lighting is exactly like it sounds-capturing footage when there is no distinct angle of the sun because the **light is being diffused by the clouds**.

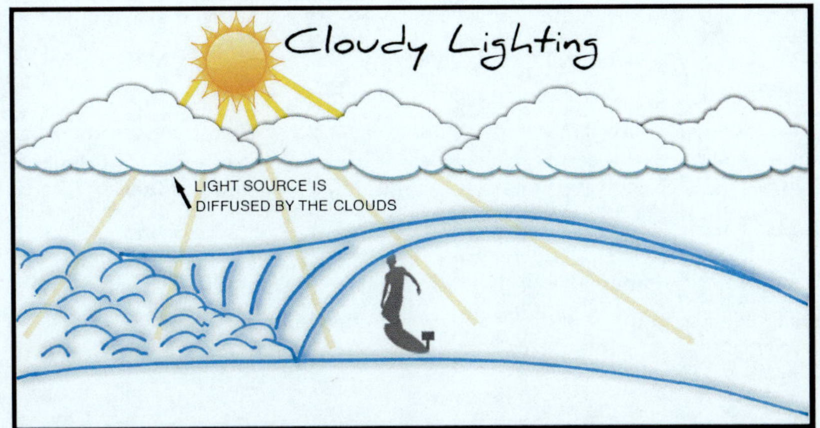

Especially when using a wide angle lens like the one on your HERO7, filming when it is cloudy gives the footage a "white" look to it, so filming in cloudy conditions is not optimal. The footage won't have the same richness and color as a sunny day, but certain shots work well in cloudy conditions.

When filming in cloudy conditions, it's also helpful to zoom in for a narrower field of view to minimize the amount of sky in your frame.

Because cloudy lighting doesn't have shadows, you can still capture usable footage if you are filming an activity that would otherwise be going in and out of shadows, like skateboarding through a city or mountain biking through trees.

High thin clouds are A LOT different than grey clouds. High, thin clouds add nice texture in the sky without diminishing the light, so if there are high clouds in the sky, go for it!

MIDDAY LIGHTING

Midday Lighting is **when the sun is nearly directly overhead**, which happens for a relatively long period throughout the middle of the day.

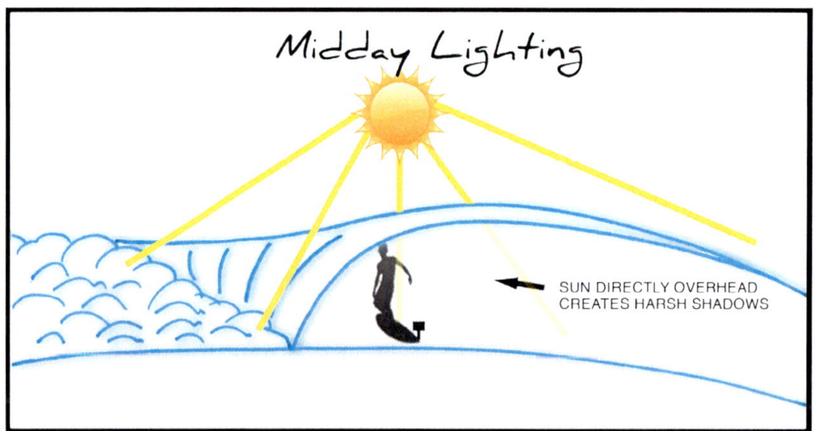

This is the worst option by almost all photographers' accounts. Harsh sun usually produces washed out colors and a lot of shadows. The best thing to do during midday lighting is to film in the shade. Or with a point of view camera, you can change the angle to minimize the harsh shadows of the midday sun. For example, a helmet-mounted position looking down works well for midday lighting.

One exception is in the ocean where the water is really clear, like in Australia, the Caribbean or Hawaii. You can actually use the midday sun's rays to your advantage in clear water because those rays create some mystical effects underwater and bring out the blue shades of the water. (See the underwater filming tips in this step for more ways to improve your underwater photography.)

FOR EXTRA DRAMATIC LIGHTING

When filming in shaded areas, for example under a canopy of trees or beneath tall buildings in the city, look for light sources that sneak through to your lens periodically in small amounts. These rays of light that come in and out of the trees or through gaps between buildings can add a lot of drama and mood to your video. For the best effect, compose your shots so the light comes toward your camera's lens. Also, a darker background creates more contrast. As you are filming, look for opportunities to let moody light enhance your scene.

When taking still photos, you can also use this type of lighting to enhance your composition. But with still photos, you can stop and let the light hit your lens in a more precise manner.

You can also add a similar effect in postproduction, using "light leak" overlays. Light leaks are slightly different, but they are commonly used as overlays to add drama to a scene. For some free light leak overlays, check out RocketStock's freebies (for Premiere Pro only). The fully functional freebies are available for free from their website.

LOW LIGHT SITUATIONS

Filming in low light situations (early morning, evening, cloudy or shady), will often create blurry photos or videos.

For the best results when you are recording video **in low light situations, do not use the Slow Motion setting (1440p-60)**. A lower frame rate (30 FPS) allows your camera to take in more light for each frame, resulting in better quality footage. The Slow Motion frame rate of 60FPS is better suited for normal daylight.

When taking photos, avoid taking Burst Photos in low light situations because your subject will often be blurred. In the standard photo mode, try to keep your camera as stable as possible when you press the Shutter Button.

TIP: Speed Blur/Motion Blur. You can **use the low light to your advantage** to create a cool, speed blur background effect. A speed blur usually has an object of focus, surrounded by scenery that appears blurred. In bright daylight, the shutter time will naturally be quick: this creates a shot where everything is in focus and appears frozen. That's perfect for shots when you want that look. This look can, however, take away from the action of the moment and make the scene look stagnant. A slower shutter doesn't freeze the action as much, and as long as you have an object of focus (usually your bike, car, or whatever your camera is mounted to), the speed blur reflects the real movement of the scene.

To obtain your subject in focus with a blurred background using Burst photo mode, keep the primary subject stationary in relation to the camera and create movement in the background.

For example, mount your camera to the front of a bike facing back at you so you and your camera move in unison. In low light situations, the camera will not have enough light to keep the moving objects in focus, giving your photos the blurred background effect. This technique works specifically well and looks really eye-catching for burst sequences but is also noticeable as motion blur in video shots.

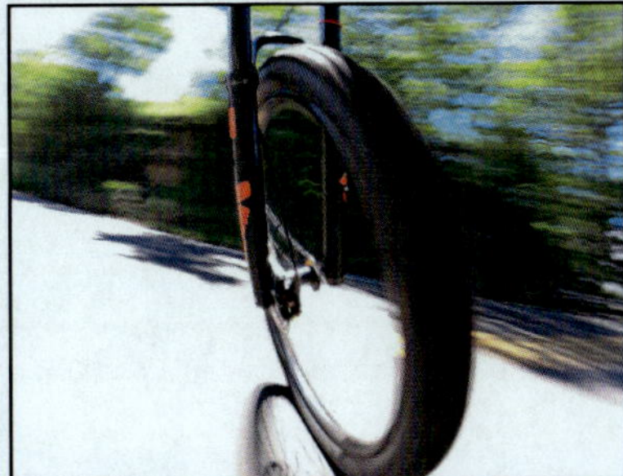

In low light situations, the slow shutter speed will blur some parts of the image. If the camera is mounted to a stationary object, the moving areas will create a speed blur

TIP: Low Light Scenes = More Noise/Grain in Your Images. When you film or photograph in low light, the camera's sensor has to compensate and absorbs light more quickly. This often results in "noisy" video and "grainy" photos.

ISO is a number used to quantify the sensor's sensitivity to light. A lower ISO (100-400) absorbs light more slowly, creating a higher quality image. A higher ISO (up to 6400) absorbs light more quickly and cannot produce as clean of images.

The Hero7 Silver/White automatically selects an ISO based on the available light, and since you can't manually set the ISO, the best way to achieve high quality videos and photos is to record in daylight. This doesn't mean you can't record in low light scenes; when you do want to record in low light, depending on the ISO selected by your camera, you can expect to see some grain in your images.

EXPOSURE

Exposure refers to the amount of light let into your camera during recording. "Correct" exposure is usually a balance between overexposed (where there is a loss of detail in the bright, highlighted, areas) and underexposed (where there is a loss of details in the darker, shadowed areas). Getting correct exposure is easiest to capture in front-lit or sometimes cloudy conditions. If you are shooting in other lighting conditions, in most situations, you will want to adjust exposure in editing software after you film.

By default, the HERO7 camera sets exposure automatically, however, **you can use Exposure Control on the Touch Screen** for tricky lighting conditions as discussed in Step 2. Exposure Control enables you to adjust exposure for a specific area of the frame rather than get an overall reading.

ACTION

For GoPro® camera users, the action often speaks for itself. Unlike traditional photography, you've already chosen your angle by the way you mounted your camera. Now it's time for you to get some great action in front of your lens. The more intense the action, the better the results.

When filming, remember to **keep your camera steady and let the action create the movement**. With video shots, a steady camera helps create footage that is easy on the eyes- too much erratic movement and it becomes hard to watch. Also, when composing shots using the Touch Screen, try to keep the horizon level.

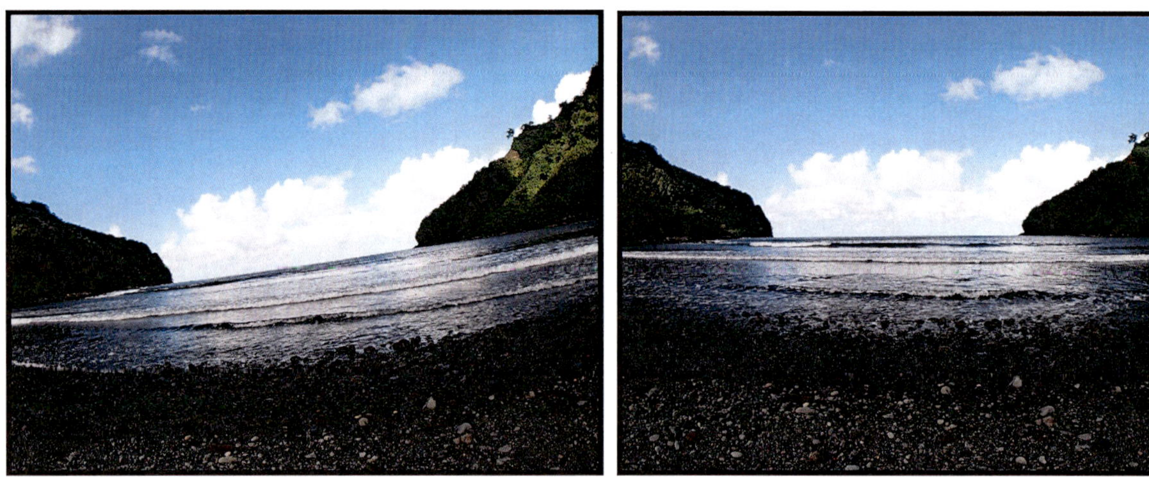

Filming with a level horizon creates a more professional-looking video.

When taking photos, a steady camera helps ensure that your photos will come out "sharp" and in-focus.

For editing purposes, it's easier to **stop recording in between "action" moments**. If it's too hard to reach your camera or your activity doesn't allow it, you can film continuously. It just means you will be searching through longer clips of footage later to find those "WOW" moments. You can also **utilize HiLight Tagging** as described below.

HILIGHT HiLight Tagging

Finding your magic moments during a video clip can send you on a long search through your files. Taking advantage of a feature called HiLight Tag might just be your solution.

When something memorable happens while you are recording, press the Mode Button on the side of your camera. Pressing this button will add a HiLight Tag. If you are using Voice Control, just say "GoPro HiLight", "Oh Sh*t", or "That was Sick". You can also add HiLight Tags while recording with the GoPro App.

When playing back video on the Touch Screen, Tap the HiLight icon on the Touch Screen to add a HiLight after the fact.

When you go to edit your video in Quik, GoPro Studio or the GoPro App, you can see the HiLight Tags on the video timeline so you know exactly where to go to find your magic moments. These HiLights also give the Quik App even more info for creating automatic QuikStories on your phone. Adding a HiLight Tag does not affect your video footage or add anything visible to the video.

FILMING TECHNIQUES

It's not really necessary for a recreational filmmaker to know the names of the various filming techniques, but an awareness of the various techniques will inspire you to add more flair to your videos. When you watch videos that impress you, pay attention to techniques the filmmaker used to make the video stand out.

Since most recreational GoPro users don't have expensive filming equipment, it's best to **make do with what you already have** to mimic these techniques in the grassroots do-it-yourself GoPro style everyone loves. The HERO7's image stabilization will help smooth out these shots, but it's still best to film them as smoothly as possible. For really smooth shots, a cheap gimbal (or the HERO7 Black with its gimbal-like stabilization) takes it to the next level.

TILT SHOT

This technique is like **looking up and then down** or vice versa. To film a tilt shot, point the camera up and then down by rotating it on its horizontal axis. This shot is typically filmed using a tripod. You can use the Tripod Mount to mount your HERO7 on a tripod if you are looking for a professional looking shot.

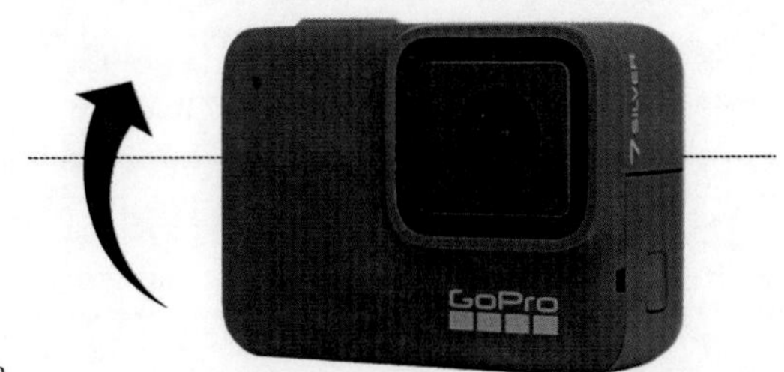

If you don't have a tripod or are on the go, you can **mimic a tilt shot** by holding your HERO7 camera with two hands while smoothly tilting the camera from top to bottom or vice versa.

PAN SHOT

A pan shot is similar to a tilt shot, except, instead of moving the camera up and down, a pan shot is **filmed in a side-to-side motion**, rotating the camera on its vertical axis from left to right or vice versa. This technique is like looking left and then right.

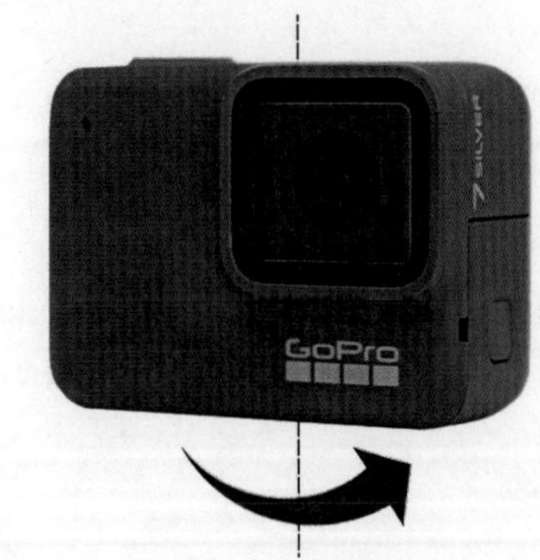

For eye-catching shots, rotate your camera from an empty scenic shot towards your subject, bringing your subject into the frame. For best results, don't pan too quickly. Also, adding a panning motion to time lapses (using the Egg Timer) adds a nice touch of movement.

DOLLY

A dolly shot is typically filmed with the camera mounted on a camera dolly, moving the **camera towards or away from the subject**.

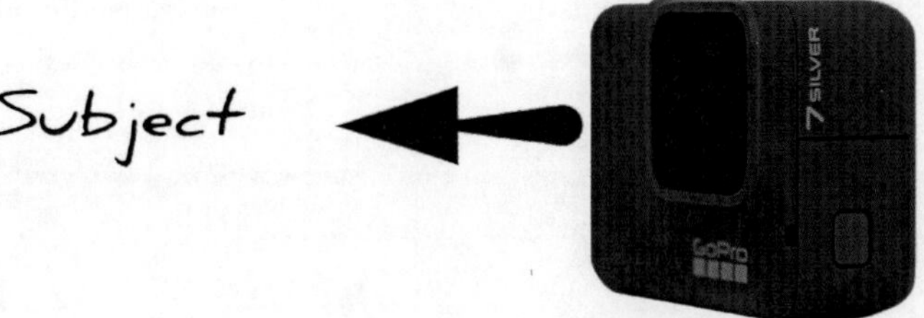

In-camera stabilization makes this shot really easy without the use of a dolly. Film your dolly shots by holding your HERO7 steady while moving your camera slowly towards or away from your subject. This filming technique looks great with stationary subjects for intros to a video.

TRACKING SHOT

In a tracking shot, the camera moves from left to right or vice versa, keeping the camera on the same axis to **move parallel with the subject.**

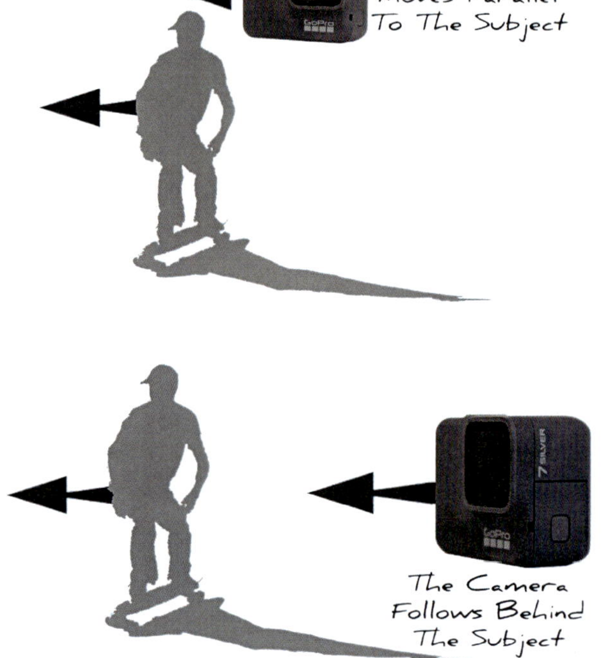

A great way to mimic this technique with your HERO7 is to hold the camera upside down on a pole or handle while riding a bike or skateboarding alongside your subject. The goal is to create smooth movement that moves with your subject. Include passing foreground objects between you and the subject for a real sense of movement.

FOLLOW SHOT

In a follow shot, the camera **physically follows the subject at a (more or less) constant distance**.

You can capture this angle of yourself by mounting your HERO7 on an extension to the back of your equipment, vehicle, etc. You can also ride behind someone on a skateboard, bike, snowboard or surfboard to follow a friend. For a steady shot, **use a polecam with your camera upside down** like shown in the Follow-Along Angle of the Handle / Polecam section.

5 IN-CAMERA VIDEO TRANSITIONS

When it comes to editing, most editing apps offer a variety of transition options to create a smooth transition from one video clip to the next, but you can really set your footage apart by filming in-camera transitions out in the field.

Typically, in-camera transitions are filmed using a gimbal to create smooth movements, however by using your most focused filming techniques, you can try to mimic these transitions without a gimbal. If you film with these transitions in mind, when you edit your clips, the hard part is already done. It just comes down to editing two clips together to make the transition happen.

TIP: When editing, use a Crossfade transition in an advanced editing app to transition from one scene to the next.

In-camera transitions are used add more flair to your quality video- kind of like a topping on your ice cream. Pick your favorites and mix them in at the beginning and end of a few of your key shots.

STRAFE BLOCK

This is probably the easiest transition to film and remember on the scene. For a strafe block transition, use a **foreground object close to the camera to blur** the end of one scene and transition to another. By filling your frame with an object (someone's body, a vehicle, a board, etc.), you can then use the same object to transition into the next clip. The key is having the same object at the next scene.

> **TIP:** With the wide angle lens on the HERO7, you will need to get close to the object you are filming to completely cover the frame. Alternatively, you can zoom in to reduce the wide angle perspective.

PUSH IN/ PULL OUT

Move in on a subject to **completely cover the frame**, and then pull out to reveal a new subject. For example, you could walk towards your subject, filling the frame with your subject's back. Then move locations and start your shot close to your subject. Pull away to reveal a new scene.

The push/pull transition is similar to the strafe block, except that it defines the camera's movement as moving in and out on a subject.

SKYFALL

Start on a subject. At the end of your shot, **tilt up to the sky**. Start your next shot aimed up at the sky. When you tilt back down, bring the viewers into another clip or scene.

WHIP-PAN

When filming in low light, you can **utilize a motion blur** to end one scene and begin another. Create a fast side-to-side motion to end a scene. In the next scene, continue that motion so you can fade in to begin the next clip.

CAPTURING AUDIO

The improved audio recording on the HERO7 lets you capture amazing high-quality footage with audio to match. The camera's internal audio recorder compiles an audio track using the two built-in waterproof microphones.

Unlike older GoPro cameras which required an external housing for waterproofing and often had muffled audio, the microphones on the HERO7 are always open for clear audio.

After you go underwater, the microphone openings tend to hold some water. **Blow them off to remove the water** from the tiny holes to capture the clearest audio possible.

Also, as with any microphones, high wind will affect the audio, but there is not a lot that can be done about that on the HERO7 since this model is not compatible with an external microphone.

UNDERSTAND YOUR LENS

The HERO7 comes with a built in Fisheye Wide Angle Lens. What does this mean? A fisheye lens is **an ultra wide-angle lens that allows more of the scene to be included in the frame**. Especially at the widest angle, fisheye lenses cause curvature around the edges of the frame.

Some corrections can be made in post-production (editing) to correct the fisheye effect in both photos and videos, but the best thing to do is learn how to work with the fisheye lens.

A Fisheye Wide Angle Lens is perfect for a GoPro camera for several reasons:

1. The camera **can be mounted extremely close to you** and still capture you in the image.

2. The lens has a short depth of field, which means **everything from about 12 inches away from the camera and beyond will be in focus**. This is great because you don't have to focus the camera.

It is important to understand the best techniques for using a fisheye lens because wide angle photography is an art in itself.

Here are some vital tips:

1. **GET CLOSE!** If you aren't close to whatever you are filming, your subject will be very small in the frame. You know how some rear-view mirrors on cars say "Objects May Be Closer Than They Appear". The same is true with fisheye lenses because they distort the perspective to make things look smaller than they look with the naked eye. Remember this and **get closer to your subject than you think you would need to**. If your subject is far away, you can crop in for a reduced fisheye effect.

2. The middle of the frame has the least amount of distortion, so **frame your images with the distortion in mind**.

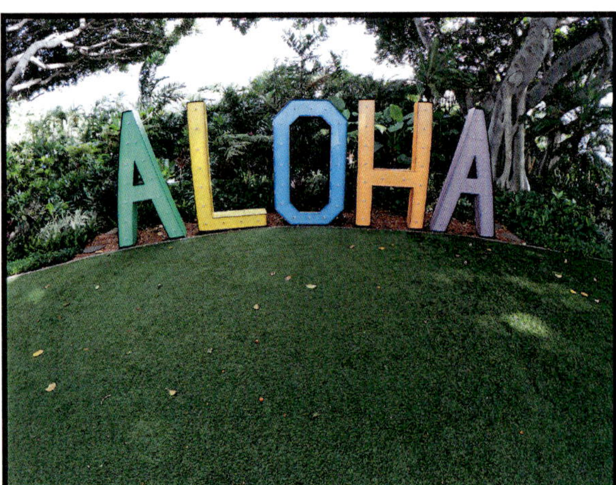

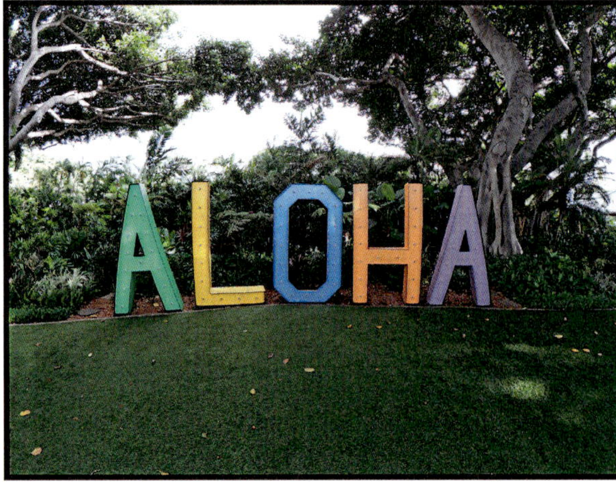

If the horizon is towards the top or bottom of the frame, it will have a curved appearance. You can remove the fisheye effect in postproduction, as you will learn in Step 5, but you also lose a bit of the content around the edges of your frame.

3. **Use the foreground to your advantage.**

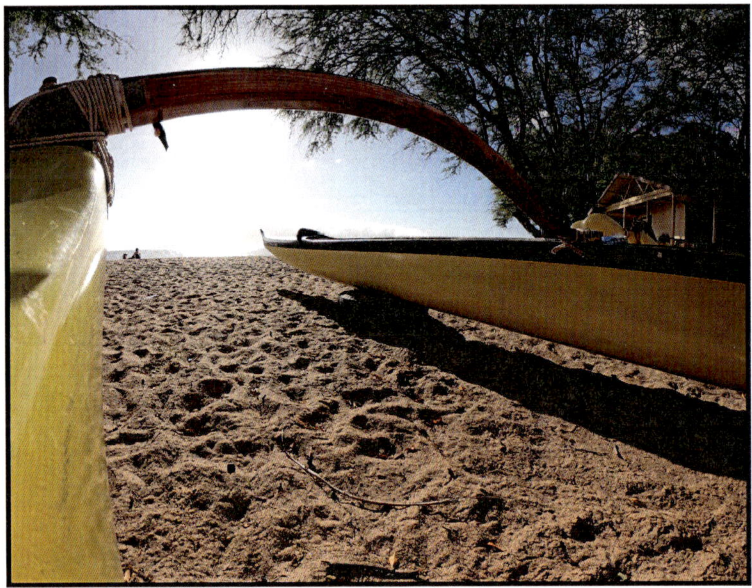

Taken on the HERO7 Silver in Photo Mode with the canoe intentionally positioned close to the camera.

By framing an object near the foreground, it will **give your image more depth**. Your arm, helmet, board, or foot make interesting foreground objects to create a sense of perspective. You can even create a cool look by "framing" your image with a foreground object.

4. **Work with the sky**, instead of against it.

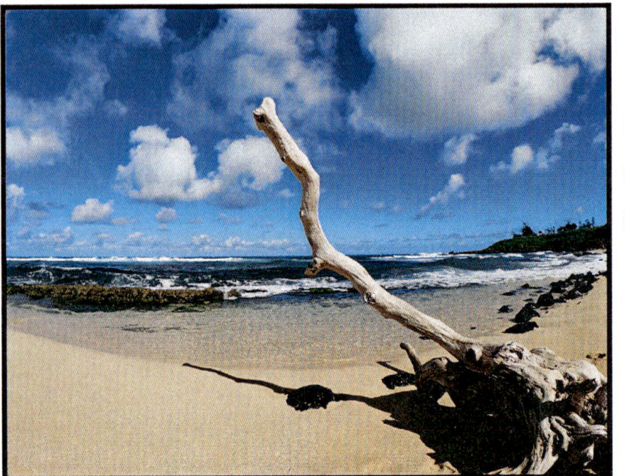

Taken on the HERO7 Silver in Photo Mode.

Because wide angle lenses capture so much in the frame, high clouds and sunset colors in the sky add a lot of drama to a scene. When the sky is gray, zoom in for a narrower FOV to reduce the amount of gray sky.

PUSHING THE SHUTTER

One last thing when it comes to capturing the action is understanding the beeps. **When taking photos in Photo Mode, the camera beeps after the camera has processed the image**. Because of this many people understandably think there is a delay.

In Burst Mode, the camera beeps one when you press the Shutter Button. Then, there is about a .5 second delay between when you press the Shutter Button and when your camera begins taking photos. It beeps while taking the 15 photo burst. Then it beeps one more time when the burst photos are processed.

An understanding of these beeps is especially useful when taking photos of people to avoid any confusion.

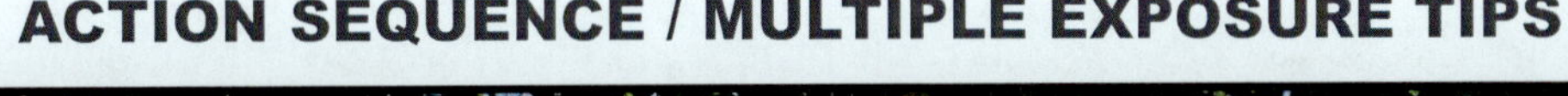

ACTION SEQUENCE / MULTIPLE EXPOSURE TIPS

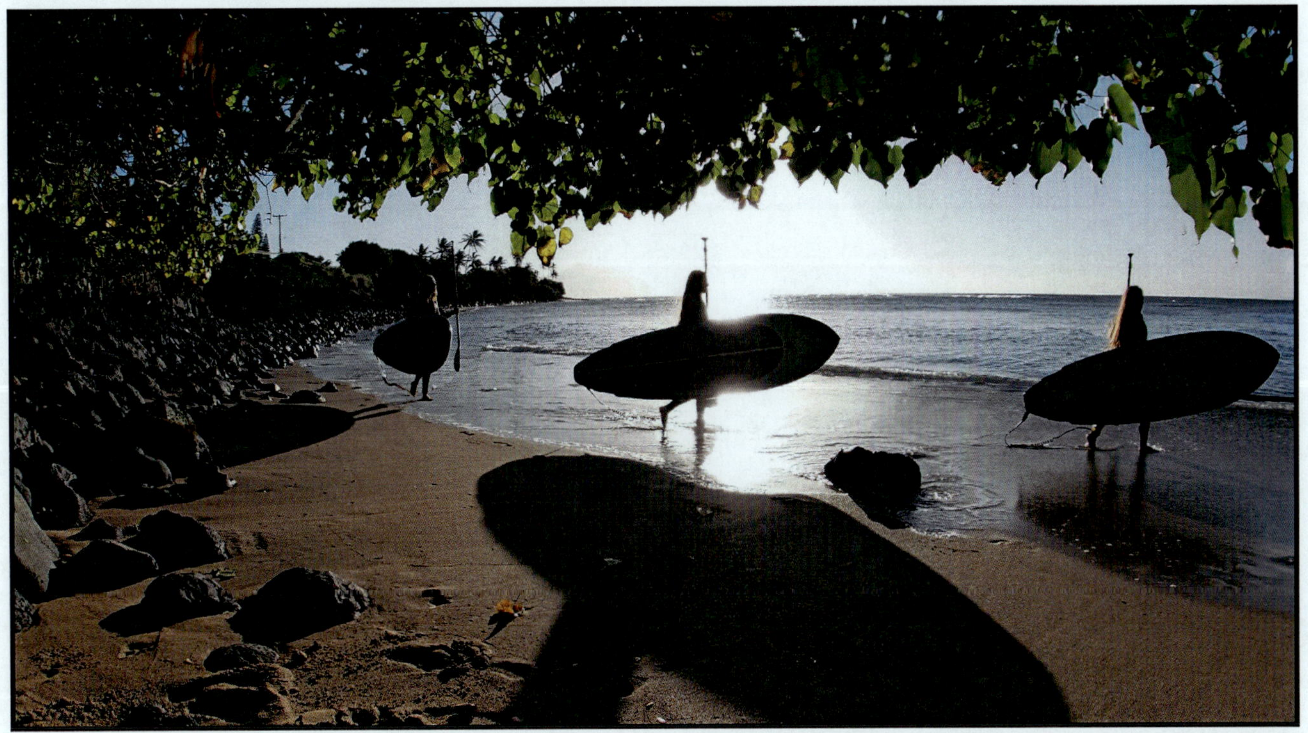

Three frames extracted from a video clip (recorded in 4k on the Hero7 Silver with the camera mounted on a tripod) were compiled into one multiple exposure photo.

An action sequence or multiple exposure is made by **editing together multiple photos to show your subject moving across the photo**. When shooting a photo sequence with the goal of creating an action sequence, **set up your shot so that your subject moves across the frame**. Pull back your camera a bit from the subject so your subject enters the scene on one side of the frame and exits on the other side. You need to have enough side-to-side distance to capture a few different images of your subject without overlapping.

For the easiest editing, **set your camera up on a tripod** or propped up on the ground so the scene remains the same and your subject is the only thing that moves.

When shooting Burst photos, there is about .5 second lag time between when you push the Shutter Button and when your camera takes the photo, so press the Shutter Button a little before the action to get your subject in the frame. With Burst turned off, you can also hold down the Shutter Button to take photos continuously for up to 60 photos.

For Burst or Continuous photos, you will need to **film in bright daylight** to give your camera enough light to take sharp photos. If your photos turn out blurry, the most common problem is there is not enough light for your camera to shoot such a fast sequence without getting blurred shots.

For **slower action**, such as hiking, or for an alternative to Burst Mode, you can **record video and pull still frames** as needed. This works especially well for self-portrait action clips so you don't have to worry about pressing the Shutter button right before the action. Also recording video will ensure that your camera continues recording until your subject has completely crossed the frame. On the Silver, record in 4k for the highest resolution files to work with.

See Step 5- Editing An Action Sequence/Multiple Exposure for step-by-step instructions on how to put together your own action sequence.

MAKE YOUR TIME LAPSES STAND OUT

In addition to using Time Lapse Video Mode to create a time lapse video, you can also speed up regular video footage for time lapse clips. Speeding up regular speed video footage to create a time lapse effect takes up more computer memory during editing and fills up your video card faster so it is not ideal for long duration time lapses. However, it can be useful for short time lapse clips. See the tip at the end of Editing a Time Lapse Video in Step 5 to learn how you can make any video look like a time lapse.

Because time lapses are time-consuming to record, when possible, set up your time lapse shot using the Touch Screen to preview the composition. If you are using an egg timer or camera slider (see below), look at the beginning shot, but also make sure the composition looks good at the end of the movement.

When recording extended time lapses, you can use an external USB power supply, like the Heavy Metal 5500 or GoPro's Portable Power Supply, to power your camera through a USB cable while you record. If using an external power supply with your camera mounted in the Frame, remove the side door for access to the USB port on your camera.

Although your camera should be mounted in a stable position when recording footage for a time lapse, adding movement gives time lapse shots a professional look. A few simple techniques can be used to create this slow-moving effect.

USE AN EGG TIMER

The Egg Timer Mount (as described in the Custom Mounts in Step 3 - Mounting) will give your time lapse shots an eye-catching rotating movement for a great panning effect.

USE A CAMERA SLIDER

A camera slider provides a smooth track to move your camera from left to right or vice versa during a time lapse.

You can make your own camera slider or buy one (they aren't cheap), but for a really good time lapse, you will need to add a mechanism for it to steadily and slowly move across the slider. For short time lapse shots, a string and some patience is one cheap and easy way to do this.

MORE TIME LAPSE IDEAS

• **Record an artist** making a drawing or a painting. A 15 minute project will play back as 1 minute of video, so longer art projects will need to be sped up when you edit.

• Mount your camera to the back of a standup paddleboard for a **downwind paddle or a bike for trail ride**. Try to get a stationary object in the foreground, like the board or a bike seat so you don't make your viewers dizzy. The moving action in the background makes for an exciting action time lapse.

• **Film the sunset at the beach or lake**. Try to choose a day with scattered clouds, and it's even better if the clouds are moving quickly through the sky. The movement of the clouds, the reflections on the water and the dwindling light will create dramatic time lapse clips. Try to frame your shot so there is some movement close to the foreground, like breaking waves or trees blowing in the wind. Because of the wide-angle lens on the HERO7, movement that is far off in the distance won't make much of an impact.

• **Film vertically.** Record a vertically oriented time lapse at 4k and edit the video into a horizontal 1080p video. When you edit, use keyframes (like you will learn about in Step 5) to transition from the top of the scene to the bottom of the scene as the video plays, creating a vertical sliding effect.

MAKE A HYPERLAPSE

• A time lapse is typically filmed from one stationary position or with very slow, steady movement. A hyperlapse, on the other hand, is filmed by moving the camera's location between every frame. To film a hyperlapse, keep your camera fixed at a certain point or object as you move. The short intervals between frames in Time Lapse Video Mode allow you to move quickly and record a lot of shots in a short period of time.

• For travel clips, film a hyperlapse as you circle around your favorite landmark or scene focusing on a central object to give your viewers a quick 360 degree view for the full experience.

• Follow behind or look back at a subject while you walk through a crowded scene. Your subject will be the only thing that seems to stay steady.

• Film your journey down a path or trail for a quick lead up to your action clips.

MAKE GOPRO CINEMATIC

One of the biggest questions new GoPro users want to know is, "How can I make my videos look more like a motion picture?" GoPro cameras have been used in many TV shows and motion pictures, although usually the Black model cameras are used.

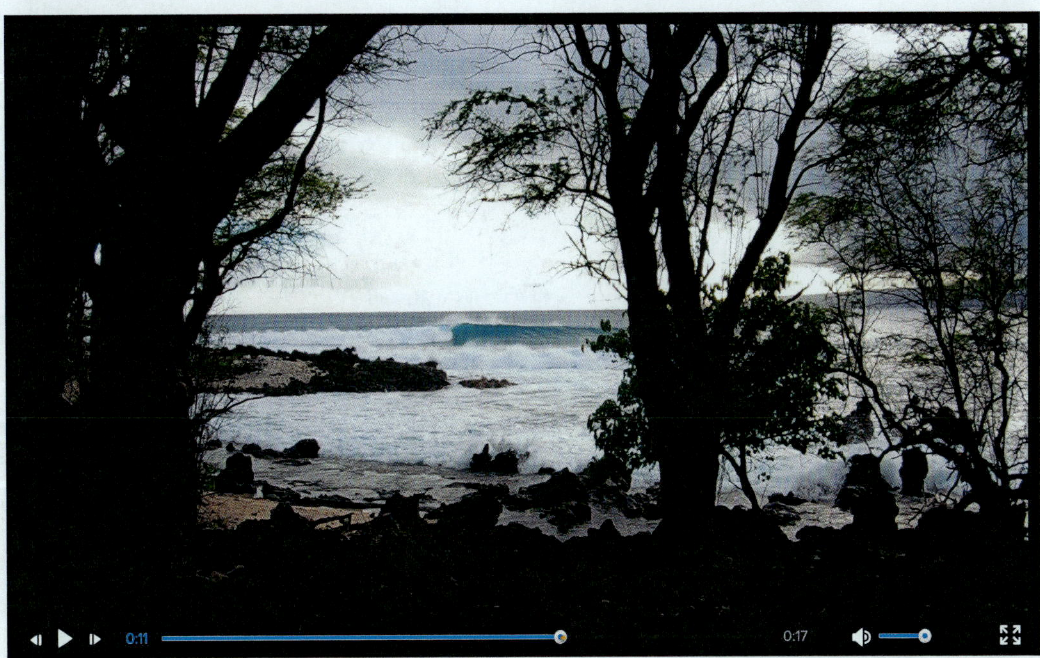

With the right settings and techniques, your GoPro footage can easily mimic cinema quality films.

Following these tips to make your video footage look cinematic:

• Take advantage of the **highest quality settings** on your camera. The HERO7 Silver offers **4k at 30 FPS** so let this be your go-to. 4k produces the highest quality images on this camera and can be brought down to 1080p with lots of extra resolution for creative editing. Also, film in bright light so the camera automatically records at a low ISO, creating the highest quality noise-free video and photos.

• To really make it look cinematic, you will probably need to export your video at 1080p. Filming in 4k (on the Silver) and exporting a 1080p video allows you to zoom in and make other framing adjustments for a more traditional-looking composition.

• Utilize **slow motion along with movement**. Use the Slow Motion setting for the creative freedom to slow down some of your key action shots. The filming techniques shown in this step, such as panning and tilting, look great with slow motion to smooth out any camera shake. If it's bumpy, it won't look cinematic.

• **Put energy into your filming**. Take your filming techniques serious and film as if you are using a bigger cinematic camera. Use a tripod if you need to and treat your camera like it's a cinema camera.

• **Film when the light is right**. Lighting makes the mood and can't be faked even with great editing. Film during the **golden hour** for mood and dramatic shadows. Use **light leaks** to let light filter in and out of your scene. The right light will make your shots look magical.

• **Film transitions.** As you film, try to remember to film a few of the creative transitions you learned in this step.

• When editing, add in **contrast** if needed to deepen the blacks. Adjust colors to get your desired look. Export your video at 24 frames per second for the most cinematic feel.

• Use **cinematic fonts** to overlay titles. Or add a logo to your intro for a professional look. There are tons of fonts available, but a few to get started that can be downloaded for free are Montserrat, Eurostile, Helvetica Neue, Bank Gothic, Couture, Nexa and Bebas Neue.

FILMING UNDERWATER SHOTS

Ahhh, the underwater world is one of the places where GoPro cameras really work their magic. Undoubtedly, you've seen amazing underwater GoPro photos and maybe you've already been inspired to capture an underwater moment like this of your own. The best underwater shots don't usually just happen without any foresight. There are a few key elements that have to be in place for these shots to work.

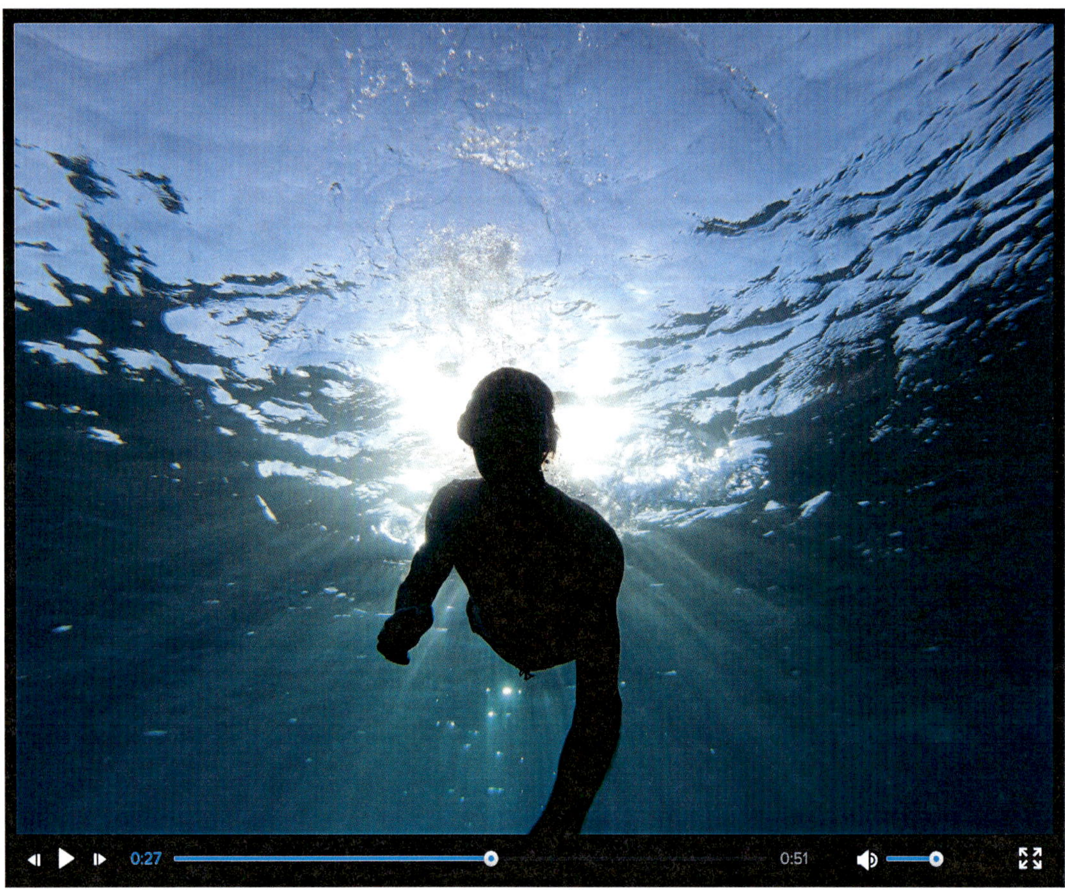

Recorded in Video Mode on the HERO7 Silver in Slow Motion (1440p @ 60 FPS) taking advantage of the late afternoon light rays piercing through clear ocean water.

• Sunny days make blue skies. **Blue skies** make great underwater photos so pick a sunny day when you can.

• You can have fun taking underwater shots any time, but **clear water** is a must-have for amazing underwater photos. The more clarity, the better your underwater shots will turn out. If there is a lot of sediment in the water, this will come between you and your subject. Not very many underwater photos you see online are taken in murky water. You can usually check water clarity at your local dive shops. Also, if the water is clear, swim rather than walk to avoid stirring up sand. It it's murky and you really want to film, get close to your subject to distract from the water clarity.

• Get close to the action, or rather **let the action come close to you**. Sea life photos often look better when the subject is coming towards the camera. Sometimes if you stay calm in the water, sea life will be curious about you and come for a closer look. Front and side angles typically look better than shots from behind. If you know you won't be able to get close, use 1080-30 and zoom in.

• **Set up your camera beforehand**. It's harder to change settings underwater, so choose your favorite settings **before entering the water**. Are you going for the expansive wide-angle view of 4k Wide (this looks great underwater)? Or do you want a zoomed in look using 1080p? Set up your video settings and photo mode settings so you can easily switch between modes and have your favorite settings ready to go.

TIP: When going in the water, make sure the side door is closed, and use a Floaty Backdoor or a floating handle in case you drop your camera. The HERO7 Silver and White are both waterproof to 33' deep.

GOPRO BASICS FOR THE TRAVELER

Thanks to its compact size and crystal-clear image quality, a GoPro camera makes the **perfect travel companion**. Capture your memories so you can bring them home with you, but remember these helpful GoPro travel tips so you score the footage without getting bogged down.

• Consolidate your gear. Even if you have a full collection of mounts and accessories (because there are lots of options), **only bring what you need**. Bring a **charger** that can be used at your destination. Figure out if a car charger, wall charger, or maybe even a solar charger goes best with your travel plans and go with that. Pick **two or three of your most versatile mounts**- preferably at least one that can record POV angles and one to film stationary shots (such as a mini tripod)- to film a variety of angles with minimal gear.

• Look at other media for an **idea of an area's highlights**. Local postcards, calendars, and artist's landscape paintings usually show an area's best attractions, so use these as inspiration. Check Instagram to see what other people are photographing in a particular area and then capture your own perspective of the sites that interest you.

• Film **using a combination of fields of view**. Zoom in for close-ups of cultural details. Mix in Wide for scenery, point of view shots, and unusual angles. Mount your camera to a moped, scooter or vehicle. A variety of perspectives in your shots will keep your audience interested longer.

• Film **Travel Hyperlapses to add excitement to your travel videos**. Film a few time lapse videos or hyper lapses of scenic highlights for extra mood. Film from the top of a tall building, near a bridge, over a river or around city lights for a different overview.

• If you have their permission, **film people** because personalities add character to a place. Or film your travel buddies to add a subject in your shots.

• **Record the sounds** of a place, such as city sounds, nature, trains, etc. Even if a scene is not visually appealing but has memorable audio that defines a place, you can record a video and choose to use only the audio track along with some other scenic clips or time lapses.

Most of all, have fun, because that will make the best videos!

TIPS TO EXTEND BATTERY LIFE

The HERO7 Silver and White use a built-in 1220mAh lithium-ion battery that should give you about 1.5 of continuous recording time in 4k (on the Silver if you don't run into overheating problems) and about 2.5 hours in other settings, depending on a few factors. Battery recording times will be less in cold weather.

The battery can be recharged by connecting your camera to a computer or USB-charging device via the included USB cable. Charging takes approximately 2-3 hours using a computer or about 2 hours using a wall charger.

You can also use the GoPro Auto Charger or Wall Charger. If you decide to use your phone's charger, the HERO7 requires a **charger that outputs 5V and 1-2A** so check your charger before you connect it to your GoPro. Using the wrong charger could potentially damage your camera.

The HERO7 is compatible with external USB power, so if you want to use an external USB power source like GoPro's Portable Power Supply or the Heavy Metal 5500, you can run off external power for an extended amount of time.

Unlike NiCad batteries, Lithium batteries don't have a memory charge, so **recharging your battery even if it is not completely drained will not reduce the battery life**.

Follow these additional tips to preserve your battery's life:

• Store your camera at a normal room temperature when possible. Try to keep your battery out of extreme heat, especially when fully charged. Keeping your camera (with the battery in it) in a hot car will deteriorate your battery's capacity.

• If you need to **store your camera for an extended period**, use it until about 40% battery life remains and store the camera in sealed bag in the refrigerator.

There are several things you can do to preserve battery life while actively using your HERO7:

• If you know you won't be filming for a while, **turn your camera off to save battery**. Your camera will go into standby mode after about five minutes of inactivity. This standby mode greatly reduces the amount of battery being used. But if you know you won't be filming for a while, it's easy to hold down the side Mode button to turn off your camera or say "GoPro Turn Off" so it doesn't use any battery life.

• **QuikCapture Mode reduces standby time** by turning your camera on and recording with one push of the button. There is a delay however while you wait for your camera to turn on, so QuikCapture Mode doesn't work for all filming scenarios.

• **Turn off the WiFi if you are not using it**. The WiFi uses some battery power to create the wireless signal. Keeping WiFi on is worth the reduction in battery life as long as you are using the GoPro App. If you are not using the GoPro App, turn off the WiFi in the Preferences>Connections dialog in the Dashboard on the Touch Screen.

• The Touch Screen uses up a good chunk of battery. If you are using the Touch Screen often and don't need it so bright, you can reduce the screen brightness in the Preferences menu. If you are primarily using the Touch Screen to set up your shots, **let the screen go to sleep after you have composed your angle** and tightened your camera in place.

Now that you have the knowledge to capture your footage, get out there and start filming! In Step 5, you will learn how to edit your photos, videos and time lapse clips!

STEP FIVE
CREATION

Now It's Time To Put It All Together

So, now you've got the footage! This should be the exciting part and with our help, it will be! There are so many fun, creative ways to edit your videos and photos! Creating your edited product is where a lot of GoPro® camera users get lost and this is why so many people have thousands of unedited photos and hours of uncut footage stored on their phones and hard drives. But it should be where you get excited because this is where you get to create! Follow this advice and you will soon be able to show everyone how much fun you are having and encourage them to get out there too!

BEFORE YOU START EDITING

TRANSFERRING FOOTAGE TO YOUR COMPUTER

To begin viewing and editing your GoPro footage, you need to transfer your videos and photos from the microSD card in your camera to your computer or phone. We will cover transferring and editing on your phone or tablet at the end of this video editing section. Many of the techniques you learn for desktop editing relate directly to mobile editing.

The easiest way to transfer your GoPro files to a computer and keep them organized is to **use the free Quik For Desktop App**.

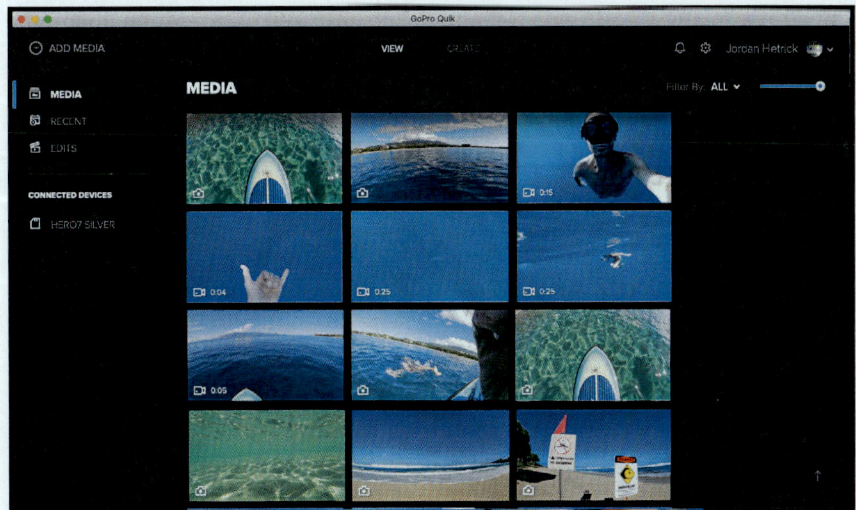

Quik for Desktop keeps your files grouped together the way you recorded them and organizes them by date. For example, if you took 60 continuous photos in Photo Mode, Quik for Desktop keeps them together as one file for organization purposes. You can still access each individual photo, but you don't have to sort through so many files to find the ones you want.

If you were to transfer these files to your computer without using the Quik App, each photo would be shown as an individual file, creating an organizational headache.

You need to set up a free User account through GoPro (with a user name and password) to use Quik for Desktop. You can download Quik for Desktop from GoPro's website at gopro.com/shop under Apps. This software works for Mac and PC.

If you sign up for a GoPro Plus account, which is GoPro's subscription cloud service, you can access your files on any computer or device (although 4k files are stored at a reduced file size- 1080p).

Make it easy on yourself and **follow the steps below** to utilize Quik for Desktop **to transfer your GoPro footage to your computer.**

Step 1: With your camera turned off, connect your camera to your computer with a USB cable. You will see a red LED light once it is connected.

Step 2: Press the Power/Mode Button on the side of your camera and Quik for Desktop **should open automatically**.

Important Note: If you are **having problems locating your microSD card** when your camera is connected to your computer, remove the card from your camera. Insert the card into the adapter and insert the adapter into the SD Card slot on your computer. Quik for Desktop will still recognize your files as GoPro files.

Step 3: An image of the HERO7 Silver or White will show up on your screen. **Click Import Media** to import your files.

Step 4: View your transferred pictures and videos. The pictures and videos you just transferred will be organized by date in Quik for Desktop. You can also use the filters at the top right to only view videos, photos or HiLights. Double-click on a video or photo to view it. Be aware that Burst photos won't preview in full resolution, but the actual files are high quality. (If you are experiencing choppy video playback, refer to the troubleshooting section at the end of this book for solutions.)

Step 5: Now you are ready to start editing.

TIP: Split Video Files. Be aware that your camera will automatically split long video files into multiple video files. Files will be split once the file size reaches 4GB. There is no interruption during recording and the time counter on your camera shows the total time recorded, regardless of how many files are created.

The reason for these split files is for compatibility with the FAT32 formatting usually used within the camera, which is limited to a 4GB maximum file size.

Split videos can be seamlessly stitched back together in GoPro Studio or any other video editing software and you won't lose any video time.

STORAGE

Your GoPro video files are going to require a lot of storage space. You will probably want to **dedicate an external hard drive to your GoPro files** (or at least a big block of memory). How much storage you need really depends on how often you use your camera, but a portable 2TB hard drive is a good starting point. Go bigger if you can. An external hard drive is the easiest way to keep your full resolution files on hand. You can also use GoPro Plus cloud storage for 35 hours of video backup at the original resolution if you are a GoPro Plus member. And remember to always back up your files to cloud storage or another external hard drive because you don't want to lose all of your hard-earned memories.

TIP: Changing the import location for your files. If you choose to use Quik for Desktop to import your files, you can set the import location to your external hard drive by selecting the Settings (Gear) icon on the top right bar of Quik for Desktop. If you move your external hard drive around from computer to computer, the files will not automatically show up in your Quik media on a different computer. To add the files to your media, Click Settings in the top right and Scan the hard drive where the new files are located.

TIP: Changing the date of files already recorded. If the date was accidentally set incorrectly, you can adjust the date after the fact in Quik for Desktop. In the top menu, select Media>Adjust Date.

DELETING FILES

To prevent the accidental loss of files, your microSD card is set as Read-Only. When your camera is plugged into the computer with a USB cable, you can copy your files from your camera into your computer's hard drive, but you do not have the ability to delete files from the microSD card. Instead, if you want to format (erase all files) from the microSD card, you can use one of the following options:

On the Camera

Using the Touch Screen:

1. Swipe Up to view your files and select the Grid Icon.
2. Select files to delete one-by-one or select all files by tapping the check mark.
3. Tap the Trash Can Icon again to delete selected files.

To format the microSD card:

1. After you have copied the files from your camera to your computer, swipe down on the Touch Screen to bring up the Preferences Menu.
2. Scroll to the bottom of the Preferences until you see the Reset option. Under Reset, tap Format SD Card.
3. The screen will ask if you want to Delete all files. Tap Delete.

Use Quik for Desktop

When your camera is connected during import, under the Settings icon next to the image of the HERO7 Silver/White, you can choose the option to "Automatically delete files from camera after importing."

Use the GoPro App

You can also copy and delete files using your smartphone or tablet.

To erase individual files:

1. With your camera's WiFi enabled and your camera connected to the GoPro App, select the GoPro Media Icon (the grid) in the App.
2. When you select a video or photo file, tap the Trash Can Icon to erase that specific file. You can erase video files, a batch of photos, or individual photos from a sequence.

To format your camera's memory card (which erases all of the photos and videos) using the GoPro App:

1. With your camera's WiFi enabled and your camera connected to the GoPro App, select the Settings Icon.
2. In the Settings Menu, under the heading Delete, you can choose to Delete the Last File or Delete All Files from SD Card.

VIDEO EDITING

VIDEO EDITING SOFTWARE

The video-editing tutorials in this chapter, Editing Your Video, Editing a Time Lapse Video and Pulling Frame Grabs, use GoPro's free editing software called GoPro Studio. GoPro stopped providing support for GoPro Studio in late 2017 because they are planning to incorporate GoPro Studio's editing features into Quik for Desktop, but these changes are still not available. Although GoPro stopped offering support for GoPro Studio, until they fully incorporate the editing tools into Quik for Desktop, **GoPro Studio still provides the best free editing option designed specifically for GoPro videos.**

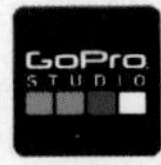

You can **download GoPro Studio 2.5 (not 2.6) for free** from third party websites. One good source for downloading GoPro Studio 2.5 is TechSpot.com. Google search "GoPro Studio 2.5 Techspot" to download the app. Make sure to download version 2.5 for the most up-to-date editing tools.

GoPro Studio does have some problems with crashing, so the best way to utilize these GoPro-specific features is to **edit a few clips at a time, save often and export them**. If you have any problems running the software, or with the software crashing, make sure your computer meets the minimum operating requirements, is running the current operating system, and has plenty of hard drive space. You can also apply most of the editing techniques in this book with other video editing apps.

For alternative free editing software and assembling longer videos, try iMovie for Mac or VSDC for Windows.

GoPro also offers two free mobile editing apps- Splice and Quik- so you can produce videos straight from your phone or tablet. You will learn how to apply your new editing knowledge to these apps as well.

PRE-EDITING IN QUIK- Creating Clips and Adding GPS Gauge Overlays.

There are several "pre-editing" tools available in Quik for Desktop to prepare your files for editing. After you double click to preview a video clip, there are **four options** at the bottom of the Quik screen.

• **Tap the Scissors Icon** to trim a video clip from a longer clip. The slider allows you to custom trim a video to any length. This will create an additional video file with the new clip and won't affect the original. For videos recorded on the Silver with GPS turned on, if you want to add overlay gauges to your trimmed clip, turn on the gauges before exporting the clip.

• The circular arrows icon allows you to **rotate your videos or photos** if needed to correct the orientation.

• Tap the image icon to **pull a still image** from your video.

• **(*Silver Only)** The fourth icon **turns on gauges,** such as Info (distance, altitude, elevation gain and date/time), Speed, G-Force, and the path you traveled. GPS must have been enabled when the video was recorded to use this feature. All of the gauges can be resized and repositioned on your video.

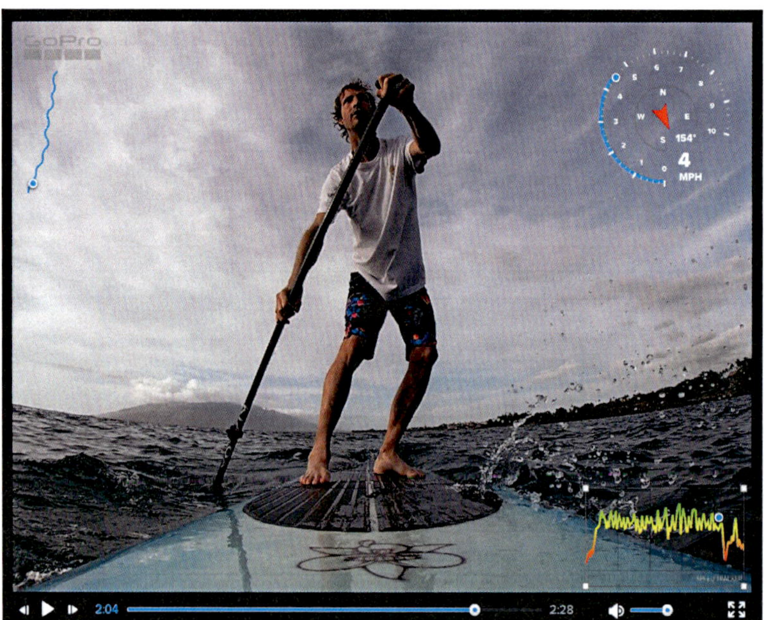

Use Quik to add GPS data overlays to your videos and Time Lapse videos.

EDITING YOUR VIDEO

This is one simple way to edit your footage. There are lots of options when it comes to video editing. But the goal of this section is to help you get your first edited clip of GoPro footage using FREE software and to understand the basics of video editing.

This video editing tutorial uses GoPro Studio because it gives you the most precise control when conforming your videos for smooth slow motion and allows you to combine clips, music and titles all within one program. You can apply this knowledge to your preferred editing app.

If you are using Premiere Pro CC or Final Cut Pro, similar editing techniques can be used and some tips for these programs will be offered throughout the editing section.

Here are some tips when you first start to think about how you are going to edit a clip:

• **Have a vision** for your finished product. If you plan to put together a video, create a storyboard or timeline to plan ahead and look for the pieces you need.

• **Bookmark** your edit worthy moments. If you weren't able to use the HERO7's HiLight Tagging feature while you were recording, you can add HiLights in Quik for Desktop as you view your videos. The HiLight tags should transfer all the way through to GoPro Studio. That way you won't have to look through hours of "in between" time for the clips you want to use.

• **Erase files as you go.** If you look through a video clip and see that there is nothing usable, erase it as you go. You will have lots of files to sort through, so the more you can thin out your library, the easier it will be to find your usable clips.

FOLLOW THESE STEP-BY-STEP INSTRUCTIONS TO CREATE YOUR FIRST EDITED GOPRO VIDEO:

#1- Select the Video Files To Use and Open Them in GoPro Studio

1. After transferring the GoPro files to your computer using Quik for Desktop, sort through your footage for two or three video clips you want to use for this tutorial. Hold Command (Mac) or Ctrl (PC) to select your desired clips.

2. With the clips highlighted, right click (Ctrl+Click-Mac) and select "Open in Studio". (This option will appear if GoPro Studio is installed on your computer.)

#2- Select Desired Clip, File Size and Playback Speed

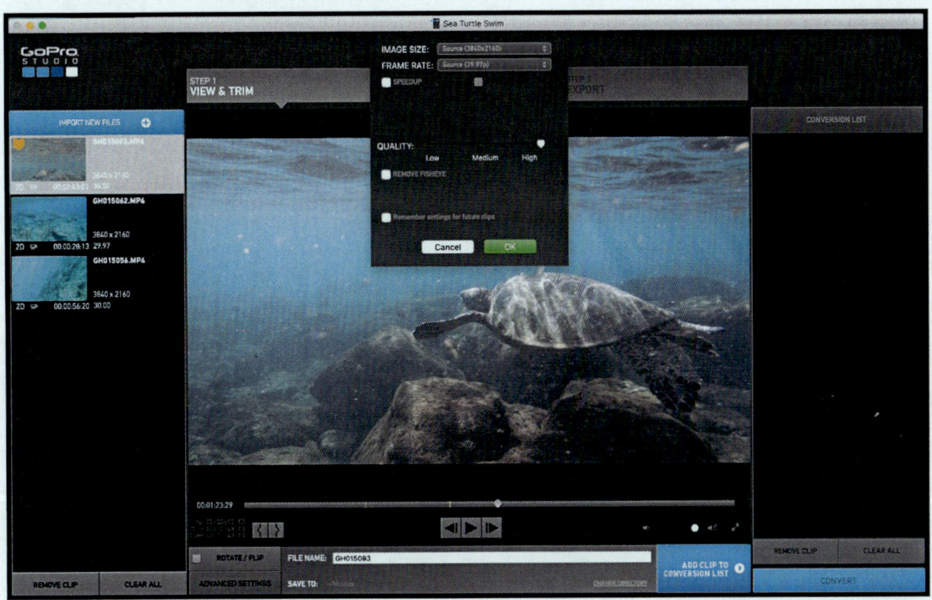

1. Save your project as you go along by clicking File>Save Project. Saving often will prevent you from losing any work if the program unexpectedly quits.

2. Click on the first clip you want to edit to bring it into the editing window.

3. If you recorded the clip upside down, you can push the Rotate/Flip box to automatically flip your footage right side up.

4. Search through the clip by pushing "Play," finding your HiLights (if you added any) or by sliding the timebar to find the "WOW" moment you want to extract.

5. Click on the "Mark In Point" below the video frame to choose where you want your clip to start. You can push pause at the exact frame you want to start with and then push the Mark In symbol. This will leave off anything before that selected point.

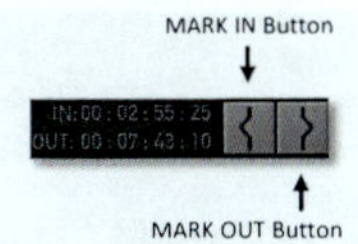

6. Play the clip or slide along the timebar and click on the "Mark Out Point" at the point where you want to end the clip. This will leave out everything after that point.

7. Click on "Advanced Settings" on the bottom left below the video clip.

8. Under "Advanced Settings", there are three settings you should adjust.

    a. Choose Image Size (for now, you can leave it at the same size it was filmed).

> **TIP:** If you change the image size, make sure to keep it in the same aspect ratio as it was filmed. Otherwise, GoPro Studio will stretch the video to make it conform to the other aspect ratio. If you prefer to crop a Standard 4:3 Aspect Ratio clip to a 16:9 Aspect Ratio, you can crop your clips in Step 2 of GoPro Studio (Read on to learn how to crop).

b. Frame Rate. If you want the clip to play at normal speed, keep it at the original frame rate. If you want the clip to play in slow motion, this is where you make it happen by choosing a slower frame rate than what you shot the footage at. If you recorded at a high frame rate and want your video to play in slow motion, try to avoid going below 24(23.98) FPS if possible. There are more advanced methods (like using Flux which you will learn about shortly) to produce ultra slow motion clips from footage recorded without a high frame per second rate.

> **TIP:** You can also adjust the playback speed of the video in Step 2, under Video, but changing the frame rate in Step 1 is a more precise way of making sure your video is playing at 24 or 30 FPS.

c. Quality- Depending on how you plan to display your clip, you should choose Medium or High.

9. Save your new clip as a new file name in the empty white box below the frame.

10. Click the blue "Add Clip to Conversion List" at bottom right.

11. Repeat steps 2-8 with the other clips you want to put in your video.

12. Click "Convert" at the bottom right.

#3- Edit the Appearance of the Individual Clips

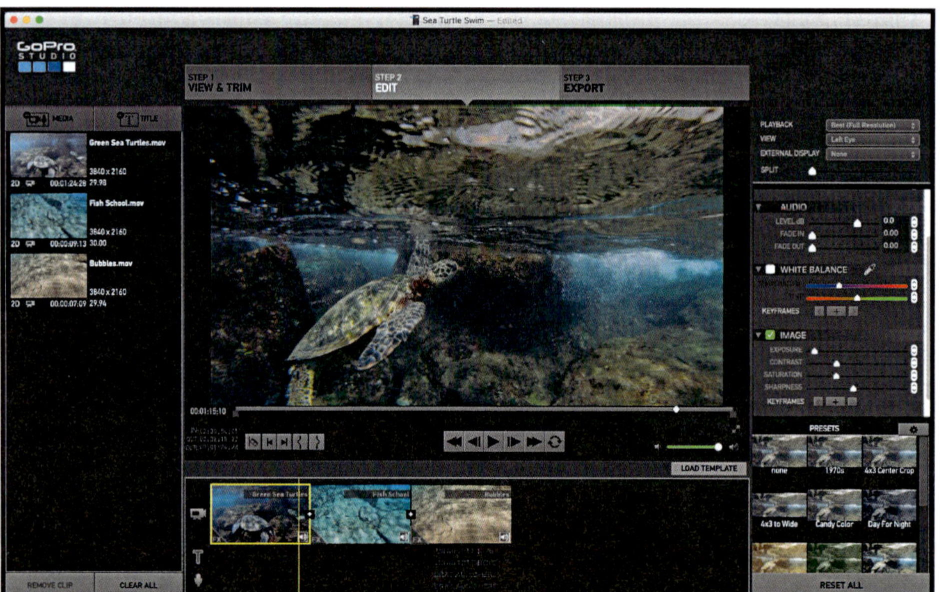

1. Click on "Proceed to Step 2".

2. When the program asks you to choose an edit template, choose "Blank Template" and click the blue "Create" button. "Step 2 Edit" on the top bar should now be highlighted.

3. In the box on the left, click on the first clip you just converted to bring it into the editing window. When you have the clip on the left highlighted, any edits you make will be to that clip. (Make sure the ProTune preset is turned off because it will oversaturate your video footage.)

4. Scroll down the tool bar on the right side and under Image, you can adjust Exposure, Contrast, Saturation and Sharpness. Be careful not to get too carried away because too much of these can make your image look doctored, especially when using the Saturation slider. You can also try out GoPro Studio's presets on the very bottom of the bar. If the colors look oversaturated to start with, under Presets choose "None" to make sure no presets were automatically applied.

5. Under "Framing Controls", you can adjust Zoom, Positioning and other options. Try these out for your knowledge and to see if any of them improve the look of your clip, but be aware that zooming in can reduce the quality of your edited footage.

TIP: Use the "4x3 to Wide" preset to conform your 4:3 Aspect Ratio (1440p) videos to 1080p with a similar look to a SuperView shot. This does not crop your clip, but rather scales and stretches it to make it fit into a Widescreen 16:9 Aspect Ratio. If you would prefer to crop your video to make it fit Widescreen without the distortion of the 4x3 to Wide preset, drag the clip to the storyboard to preview it in a Widescreen Aspect Ratio. Then, in the Framing dialog box, adjust the Vertical slider until you are happy with the cropping.

6. When finished editing the appearance of your clip, move on to the next clip until you are happy with the appearance of the clips.

#4- Combine Clips, Add Music and Put Together your first Movie

1. To combine your clips, select each clip from the box on the left and drag the clips in the order you want them into the storyboard below. Drag them to the right of the video camera icon (where it says, "Drag Video Here"). You can rearrange the order by dragging the clips in the storyboard.

2. If you find the clips are too long or have unnecessary parts, you can fine tune the start and stop points for each clip from within the storyboard by using the Mark In and Mark Out Points button.

TIP: **Multiple Speeds.** After dragging your clip into the storyboard, split the clip and speed back up certain parts to create more exciting action. Find a point of the clip where you want to speed back up the action and click on the "Split Clip at Current Position" button (to the left of the "Mark In Point" button) to split the clip. This will split the clip into two pieces. Then, click on the portion of the clip you want to speed back up, and in the Video dialogue on the right side, adjust the speed. if you converted videos shot at Slow Motion (60 FPS) to 30 FPS in Step 1, 200% will bring your clip back to normal speed. By speeding up certain parts, you can make the slow motion parts more dramatic and impactful.

TIP: Reverse Motion. You can play your video in reverse by clicking on the "Reverse" box under the Video dialogue. To make it exciting, drag a clip into the storyboard twice and play the second one in reverse so the action plays back on itself.

3. Add transitions in between the action clips for a more professional look. Click on the "+" sign in between each clip to change it from a cut to a dissolve. (iMovie, VSDC and most other editing apps offer more transition options).

4. Add some titles to the beginning and end. Click the "+ Title" icon at the top of the left bar. When you click on the title "clip" that you just added in the bar to the left, you change the title text and appearance on the right side. Fill in the text in the preview box on the right to give it a title (Snowboarding Chile, e.g.). Once you are happy with the words and appearance, you can either: Drag the title "clip" onto the Video bar in the storyboard before the first clip for it to be a title screen on its own OR Drag it into the Title bar on the storyboard for it to show up over the video clip.

5. Add music to create the mood. At the top of the box to the left, click the Media icon to the left of the "+Title" icon. Add a song from your computer and drag the song into the Audio bar of the storyboard. You can adjust the length of the song by clicking on the song in the storyboard and dragging the end to match the end of your video clips. If you don't want the original audio from the video clips in the background along with the music, you can click on the audio icon that is on the video clip thumbnail in the storyboard to turn off the clip's audio.

6. Press the Spacebar to preview your edited movie and make any changes.

7. When you are happy with your edited video, click on Step 3: Export. This will bring up the export dialogue.

• If you edited a Widescreen 16:9 video, under the Presets, select HD 1080p or HD 720p and export the finished video.

(*Silver Only)

- To export 4k video (for footage filmed in 4k), select Custom and under Image Size, select 4k.
- To export video at a Standard 4:3 aspect ratio, under the Image Size tab, select Source.

You now have your first edited GoPro® video clip!

> **TIP: Preparing Files For YouTube.** When producing videos for YouTube, you can upload either 1080p or 4k (called 2160p on YouTube) resolution videos. The YouTube uploader will automatically detect your video resolution and give viewers resolution options to suit their device.

> **TIP:** If you want to get even deeper into how GoPro Studio Software works, go to GoPro.com and under the Support Tab>Product Manuals>Software, you can access a pdf version of the GoPro Studio manual. The Studio Manual has tons of helpful information.

*After you become comfortable with GoPro Studio, you may want a professional program like Final Cut or Premiere with more capabilities, but to begin with, GoPro Studio will give you a good intro into video editing.

> **TIP: MUSIC.** When putting together a video for YouTube, you must have permission to use music. A few sites give you permission to use their songs for free (they usually ask that you give them song credits in exchange for the free music). Try out these sites which offer some free songs to use for your videos if you plan to upload them to YouTube:
> http://incompetech.com
> http://www.melodyloops.com
> http://freemusicarchive.org
> YouTube also has a selection of free songs under Creator Studio>Create>Audio Library.
> Or you can buy songs at stock sites like iStock.com (they also have a free download every week if you sign up for an account).
> For sound effects, try:
> https://www.freesound.org
> http://soundbible.com/royalty-free-sounds-1.html

GO DEEPER

MORE EDITING TECHNIQUES

Once you are comfortable with the basics of video editing, check out the options below for some extra effects.

SUPER ULTRA SLOW MOTION VIDEO USING FLUX

As you learned previously, to achieve true slow motion, you are limited to the frames that were actually recorded in the original video. For example, when you conform video recorded at 60 FPS down to 30 FPS, you can only slow down the footage 2x to maintain smooth video footage. When using the Speed slider bar in Step 2 of GoPro Studio, that is 50% of the original speed.

With Flux, you can slow your footage down to 3%-10%, so **you can achieve super ultra-slow motion** far slower than the original frame rate would allow. This creates an almost paused effect.

However, not all is perfect with the Flux option. To achieve super slow motion, Flux makes up frames that don't exist by analyzing the frame before and the frame after and then fills in the space with digitally-created frames. For some scenes, this works really well, and for others, the results are far less than perfect.

Consider the following tips when you want to edit your clips into ultra-slow motion:

• When possible, **record at a high frame rate** so that Flux doesn't have to create so many frames. The fewer frames Flux has to digitally create, the better your chances for an effective result. However, Flux can be used with footage recorded at any frame rate.

• Choose the right scenes to apply Flux to. **Clean backgrounds and simple scenes** work better because they are more predictable. Flux really works best when the subject is against a plain blue or grey sky. Busy scenes with lots of background elements, such as bushes or water, make it harder for Flux to imagine what the missing frames should have looked like. You can try Flux out with any clips, but if the results come out strange, the background could be the problem.

• Choose the right section of the clip to apply Flux. Flux is best applied **when the subject is above the horizon**, so split the clip when the subject goes above the horizon and split the clip again before the subject comes back down. The resulting section would be the best bet to slow down for a successful application of Flux.

• GoPro recommends **slowing the footage to 3%-10% for the ultra-slow motion sections**, but Flux can be applied to any video that has been slowed down using the Video Speed slider bar in Step 2 of GoPro Studio.

TO APPLY FLUX:

1. In Step 2 of GoPro Studio in the section on the left side, click on the thumbnail of the desired clip and drag the clip to the Storyboard.

2. Find a short section of the clip you want to play back in super slow motion. It's best to isolate a short 1-3 second clip because when you slow it way down, the clip becomes a lot longer.

3. Split the clip before and after the section you want to slow down by dragging the slider to the points you want to clip and pressing the Split Clip icon on the left side above the Storyboard.

4. Make sure the clip you want to slow down is highlighted and under the Video tab on the right side, drag the Speed Slider to the left to reduce the speed of the video. When you drag the slider the Flux option will appear. Leave this box checked for the clip or clips where you want Flux applied.

5. Export your video. On the export dialog, there is another option to Apply Flux. Leave this box checked to apply Flux and export your video.

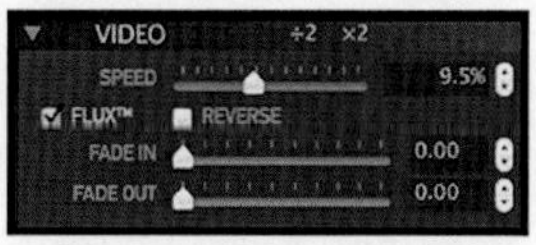

NOTE: Exporting with Flux applied takes considerably longer because GoPro Studio has to analyze and create new frames, so make sure you only apply Flux to the clips that need the extra frames.

TIP: A similar effect can be applied in Premiere Pro or Final Cut using "Optical Flow" time interpolation.

REMOVE THE FISHEYE EFFECT

The wide angle lens on the GoPro causes some curvature around the edges of the frame. Some people prefer to **reduce the amount of fisheye effect in their videos**. Unfortunately, since GoPro has stopped updating GoPro Studio, removing fisheye from HERO7 videos in GoPro Studio isn't as easy as it was for earlier camera models. However, there is still a way to remove the fisheye appearance from the wide angle lens using GoPro Studio.

The "Remove Fisheye" box in Step 1 of GoPro Studio will appear in the conversion dialog, but unfortunately, **this won't fix your HERO7 videos**.

Although it's not as effective as using advanced editing apps such as Final Cut Pro or Premiere Pro, the best way to remove fisheye from your videos in GoPro Studio is to **use a combination of Framing controls**. In the Framing dialog in Step 2 of GoPro Studio, there are three sliders you can use to reduce the fisheye effect. First, use the H.Zoom and H.Dynamic sliders in combination to reduce the fisheye effect. These will stretch out the center of the frame to reduce the "bubble" in the middle.

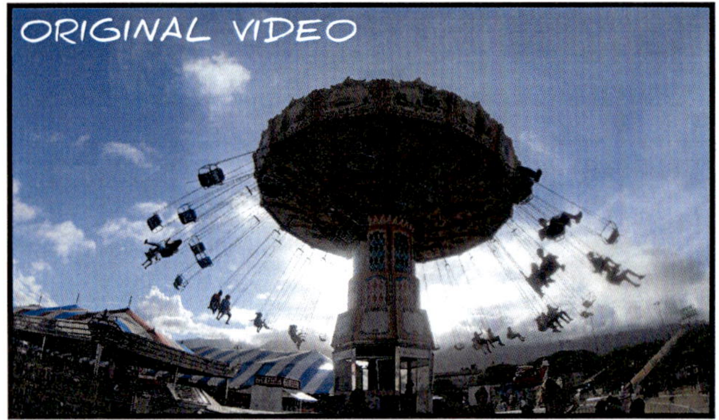

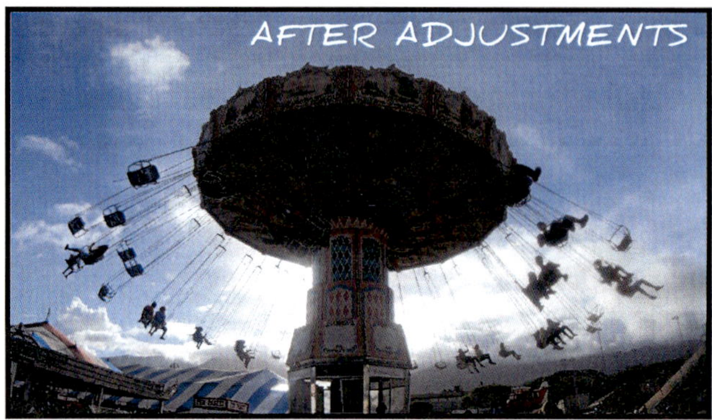

The original image was filmed in Wide FOV. H.Zoom and H. Dynamic framing adjustments were applied to the middle image to reduce the fisheye effect.

If you want even more of a reduced fisheye effect and can spare losing some of the content around the edges of the frame, after adjusting your image using H.Zoom and H.Dynamic, use the Zoom slider to zoom in and crop the edges out of the frame. If you are editing to a lower resolution than the recorded video resolution, you have enough extra resolution to zoom in and still maintain high res video. For the Silver, if you filmed in 4k and are making a 1080p video, you can zoom in 200% without losing resolution. In GoPro Studio, these percentages need to be estimated because there is not a percentage marker in the Zoom slider.

TIP: ADVANCED EDITING: For more accurate fisheye removal, use advanced editing apps. In Premiere Pro, use Lens Distortion>Curvature in Effect Controls to reduce fisheye. In AfterEffects, use Optics Compensation. In Final Cut Pro, use the Fisheye filter, or the free Alex4d Wide Angle Fix plugin.

USE KEYFRAMES TO ADD EFFECTS

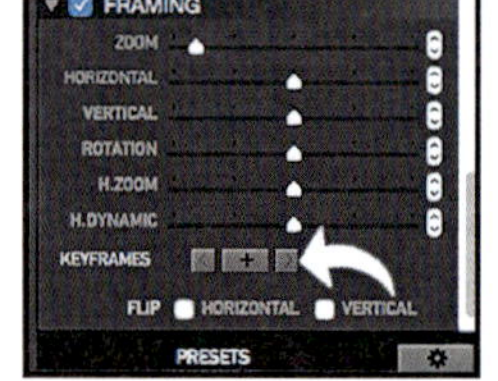

Use Keyframes to add changing visual effects within a video, or to create movement in a stationary scene, such as panning or zooming. A keyframe is used to make a marker of any of the visual settings, including, Saturation, Exposure, Contrast, etc. as well as Framing Controls like Zoom, Horizontal, Vertical, etc. The video then smoothly transitions from the effects applied in one keyframe to the next.

Keyframes buttons in GoPro Studio are located in the White Balance, Framing, and Image dialog boxes on the right side.

To add Keyframes to your video:

1. In Step 2 of GoPro Studio, drag your clip into the Storyboard.
2. In the Storyboard, move the Time Indicator to the beginning of the clip.
3. In the Image Settings>Framing, click the + button next to Keyframes. This will add a Keyframe at this point for adjustments made to that dialog box.
4. Make any visual adjustments you want to make at this Keyframe.
5. Move the Time Indicator to a point later in the clip.
6. Click the + button next to Keyframes. This will add a Keyframe at this point.
7. Make any visual adjustments you want to make at this Keyframe.
8. Play the video and watch the transition from the first Keyframe to the last.

For example, you can use keyframes to move across the frame of a scenic shot. To mimic a panning effect, first Zoom in on the scene. Use horizontal controls to add a Keyframe at the beginning of a time lapse clip showing the left side of the frame. You can then add another Keyframe at the end of the time lapse showing the right side of the frame. The video will then transition from the first keyframe to the last as the video plays, creating a panning effect.

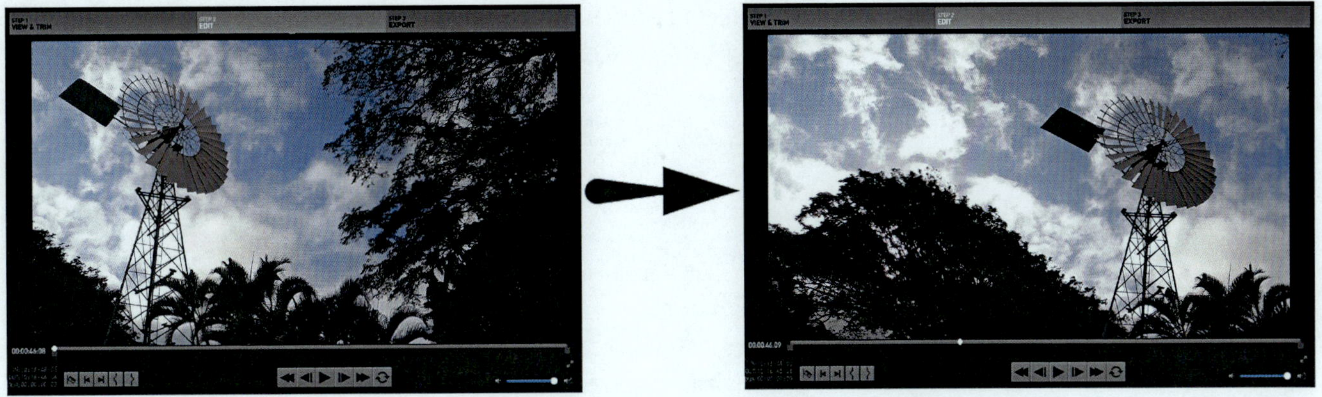

Use keyframes to pan across an image, adding a sense of movement to a stationary shot.

You can also use keyframes to mimic a zoom shot. If you filmed in 4k on the Silver, zoom in to an object such as a moonset over the ocean. Since your GoPro doesn't zoom while filming in Slow Motion or 4k (on the Silver), you can use keyframes to create a zoom shot.

To mimic a zoom shot, add a Keyframe at the beginning of a full frame clip. Then zoom in and add another Keyframe at the end of the clip. The video will then transition from the first keyframe to the last as the video plays.

CREATE A CINEMAGRAPH/PLOTAGRAPH

Cinemagraphs are a relatively new media creation- basically a **fusion between a photo and a video**. In a cinemagraph, most of the scene appears stationary as you would see when viewing a photo. The magic of a cinemagraph is that a selected part of the image shows movement.

Imagine a beautiful sunset photo, with all of its colors to appreciate, but in this scene just the ocean and one palm tree are moving in the breeze. These kinds of imaginative scenes can be created using a cinemagraph technique.

Cinemagraphs are generally short, with the moving areas set to "loop"- play over and over. Cinemagraphs can then be used on websites or social media.

There are **two ways to make a cinemagraph**- the first is to create one manually using an advanced video editing app, such as Premiere Pro, Final Cut, or even Photoshop. There are several helpful tutorials on YouTube if you search for "Cinemagraph Tutorial". Once you learn the technique, you will be able to create these to your heart's content.

The second method is to use Flixel, which is easy, but requires a paid annual subscription. Flixel allows you to easily create cinemagraphs and also provides hosting so you can easily share the results.

Tips for Creating a Cinemagraph

• Use a tripod. A stationary shot makes it easier to expose the moving areas through the still image.

• When planning your cinemagraph, envision which area you will use to reveal movement.

• When editing, make sure some of the frozen areas are areas that would naturally contain movement, so the viewer can easily recognize the effect.

Plotagraphs

A plotagraph is similar to a cinemagraph. The difference is that a plotagraph begins with a still photo, not a video. An area of the photo (the sky, for example) is then animated by digitally adding looping movement. Plotagraphs are also very popular on Instagram and websites because they are easier to create than a cinemagraph. The easiest way to create a plotagraph using your GoPro photos is to use a free app on your device called Enlight Pixaloop or Plotaverse.

TIP: Fix your Footage. Sometimes footage doesn't come out like we hope for. Fortunately some things can be corrected after the fact. Here are a few common filming mistakes you can fix in editing

• **Underexposed shots.** If you filmed in low light, your footage may be darker than desired. You can brighten the exposure in any editing app to lighten the shots, but make sure you don't go too far because it may bring out noise in your shots.

• **Shaky video.** For shots that came out shaky, playing your videos back in slow motion helps to butter up shaky shots.

• **Audio.** If your video's audio track is less than par, you can first try to correct it using audio filters in a video editing app. The other option may be to mute the track's original audio and record a voiceover, use a separate sound effect audio track, or use that clip with music as the audio.

EDITING A TIME LAPSE VIDEO

A time lapse is a fusion of photos and videos because you are capturing the scene through a long sequence of spaced out images, but you play back the scene at the rate of a regular video. Time lapses are fun, creative additions to any video and they can give your viewers a great understanding of the overall scene.

The easiest way to edit a time lapse or hyper lapse is directly in GoPro Studio because of its simplicity and quality.

(Note: Time Lapse Videos automatically play at 30 frames per second)

Editing Tips:

• See something you don't like in one of the frames of a time lapse sequence? You can split the clip and cut the frame out using GoPro Studio without noticing it in the edited video.

• In Step 2, you can **edit the appearance** of the time lapse video like you did in the Editing Your Video tutorial. Adjust the speed, exposure and other settings using the dialogue boxes to the right.

• Work with the speed. Try **adjusting the speed** in the Speed slider on the right to get the look or length you are going for. This is especially useful for longer duration events that would benefit from a longer interval.

• As you learned earlier, you can **use keyframes to add extra movement**, such as panning or zooming, to your time lapse. This is especially effective for videos that are being exported to a lower resolution than the original recorded video (eg, 4k to 1080p or 1080p to 720p).

• Depending on your computer's speed, your time lapse may not play back smoothly until you export it. The preview doesn't show all of the frames, so it will look choppier than the final exported video. **Export your video to view the full effect of your time lapse**.

• If you want to conform a 4:3 aspect ratio time lapse to Widescreen 16:9, use the 4x3 to Wide preset. If you would prefer to crop your time lapse to make it fit Widescreen without the distortion of the 4x3 to Wide preset, make sure the clip is in the storyboard and in the Framing box, adjust the Vertical slider until you are happy with the cropping.

TIP: Time Lapse From Video. You can also simulate a time lapse look from a regular video clip using GoPro Studio. In Step 1 of GoPro Studio, click on Speed Up under Advanced Settings. When you click on Speed Up, a slider will appear with a box to insert a number, indicating how many frames you want to remove. A higher number will skip more frames and speed up the motion. You can also click on Motion Blur once Speed Up is checked to give your time lapse a blurred effect in between frames.

MOBILE EDITING APPS- SPLICE AND QUIK

Mobile video editing is easy and convenient for sharing short clips, but you will still probably want to use a computer for longer edits or high-res 4k footage. Transferring and editing files takes longer on a phone or tablet, and, depending on your phone's capability, the resolution output is generally lower. But, it's still fun and convenient to edit and share your footage on the go!

GoPro offers **two free mobile video editing apps** so you can easily make edits on your phone or tablet. The two apps are Quik and Splice. Splice is currently only available on iOS. Quik is available through the App Store (iOS) and Google Play (Android).

To edit your GoPro footage in Splice or Quik, the **files you want to edit must be saved to your phone**. Save videos to your phone by using the GoPro App and downloading the files you want to use. You can also access files on your microSD card by using the Quik Key, which is a mobile card reader made by GoPro. If you are using an Android phone with a microSD card slot, you can insert your camera's card and access your files this way as well.

QuiK STORIES

AUTO EDITS USING QUIKSTORIES

Quik Stories makes it easier than ever to share your GoPro content. Quik Stories uses WiFi/Bluetooth to **automatically transfer your recent photos and videos from your GoPro to your device** and edits them into a short video with music. The video can then be instantly shared or edited further.

• Footage captured within two hours of each other are edited into one Quik Story. Multiple Quik Stories may be automatically edited, depending on how much footage you filmed in the previous 72 hours. Make sure you have enough storage to transfer files to your device.
• QuikStories will transfer videos, single photos and time lapse videos, but not burst photos.
• All of the transferred footage will remain on your camera's memory card.
• Automatically transferred files can be accessed in the Media section of the GoPro App. After 7 days, those files will be deleted from the App unless you save them to your phone's media.
• If you are filming with the intention of making a QuikStory, shorter clips at 1440p/1080p transfer much faster than longer clips or higher resolution video. If the video resolution is incompatible with your device, the GoPro App will automatically convert files to a lower resolution.

How To Use Quik Stories

1. To make a QuikStory, make sure the camera has been connected to the App previously.
2. Turn on your GoPro's Wi-Fi and Bluetooth (turn on Wireless Connections under Connections from the top tray)
3. Launch the GoPro App and Swipe Down on the home screen of the App to search for photos or videos shot within the last 72 hours.
4. The GoPro App will automatically transfer recent files and edit them together. When your edited video is ready, the App notifies you that "Your QuikStory is ready!"
5. Tap "Get It" to go into Quik, which is GoPro's automated mobile video editing app.
6. Open Quik to preview your edited video. The edited video might turn out exactly how you want it, or it may just be a starting point for you to begin with.
7. For further editing, use the Quik editing tools that you will learn about next to remove unwanted clips and adjust highlights.
8. Once you are happy with the video, you can share your clip via apps (depending what apps you have on your device), messages, email, copy the link or add it to your photo library.

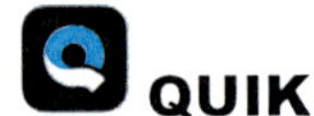

QUIK

Quik is just like the name says- **a great tool for making quick edits** that are virtually automatic. Quik doesn't offer a full toolbox of editing tools like Splice does, but if you want an easy way to combine videos and photos, add filters by theme and throw some music in there, Quik will get the job done for you. As you just learned, Quik is used to edit your QuikStories. Quik can also put together an automatic weekly video of your footage.

Quik has the following tools to choose from:

• **Style-** Choose a video style based on Quik's pre-designed themes. The style can be changed instantly on your edit simply by selecting a different style.
• **Music-** Add music to your video. Choose from GoPro's library or add music from your phone's library.
• **Settings-** Choose the pace, which will change the speed of how fast elements are displayed one after the other. Choose the format, which can be Square or Widescreen (Standard 4:3 videos will be cropped to Widescreen). You can also delay the music to start later in the video. And last, but not least, you can add filters (and adjust the intensity) to the overall video for a united look. There are 20 filters to choose from:
4 Beach Filters- Keel, Waimea, Vibe and Soleil
4 Indoor Filters- Nola, Grotto, Vegas and Asana
3 Snow Filter- Bluebird, Aspen and Luge
3 Urban Filters- Rooftop, Graffiti, and Grind
4 Vegetation Filters- Zipline, Sequioa, Vail and NaPali
and 2 Water Filters- Gili and Ibiza

But that's not it- there are more editing options available depending on what type of clip you are editing- either a Title slide, a video clip or a photo.

To edit title text slides, individual video clips, or photos, Tap the screen and then the pen icon to enter the editing dialogue.

When editing a **Title Slide**, the four editing options at the bottom of the screen are:
• **Text-** Edit the title text or add title slides.
• **Delete-** Delete a title slide.
• **Duration-** Adjust the length of the title slide.
• **Duplicate-** Duplicate the selected title slide.

When editing a **Video Clip**, the following tools are available:
• **Text-** Add a text overlay on your video.
• **Delete-** Delete the selected clip.
• **Hilight-** Hilight your favorite parts of a video for Quik's auto editing.
• **Trim-** Trim the beginning or end of the clip to select the area you want included.
• **Adjust-** Rotate videos if the orientation is off. Videos can also be repositioned to adjust the crop, which is especially useful for 1440p Standard 4:3 Aspect Ration videos.
• **Volume-** Adjust the video's audio volume.
• **Speed-** Adjust the playback speed of your clip to Slow (if you filmed at 60 FPS), Regular or Fast.
• **Fit-** This will show the full view of the clip, which may create black bars at the top and bottom for Standard 4:3 Aspect Ratio videos.
• **Duplicate-** Duplicate the selected video clip.
• **Speedometer** (*Silver Only- If GPS was enabled)- turn this on to display your speed.

For **photo editing**, two additional options are available:
• **Focus-** Determine where you want to set the focus to add a filter to the photo.
• **Duration-** Set the video duration of the photo to Long, Regular or Short.

Once you have finished editing in Quik, save your video to your photo library or share it through Social Media outlets.

SPLICE (iOS ONLY)

Splice is a mobile video editor that offers **much of the freedom and creativity of a desktop video editing app**.

Now that you know the basics of video editing, you can apply that knowledge to Splice. Using the editing techniques you just learned for GoPro Studio, you can make video and photo compilation edits with a variety of transitions, titles and audio.

Just select your media from your device's photo library and add them to the storyboard. You can also use files from your DropBox, Facebook, Google, Instagram or GoPro Plus. From the storyboard, you can edit the individual clips, add audio and titles, change the transitions and produce a quick and easy video of your event.

Splice has the following tools to choose from:

Trim/Cut- Trim the ends off your video or cut parts from the middle of your clip.

Wand Tool (Filters)- Apply filters to your videos or photos. Some examples include Warming, Blue, Noir (black and white), and Sepia.

Speed (for videos)- Adjust the playback speed for slow motion or speed up your videos. To avoid ending up with choppy video, the same rules about slow motion frame rates apply here.

Titles- Add title pages to your video or subtitles on your clips.

Motion- Crop your images or add a Ken Burns effect (slow pan and zoom) to your videos and photos.

Audio- Add voiceovers, music and soundtracks to your video. You can adjust your clip's audio, as well as add two tracks of music and a voiceover.

When you finish editing, there are a variety of ways to share your edited video directly from the app, including sharing a link, saving the video to your device or uploading it to your favorite social media.

> **TIP: More editing apps.** There are a few other mobile video editing apps you may find useful. Chromic has some nice color grading tools. Post Edit is similar to Splice but you can also overlay a drawing on the video or add sticker graphics. Adobe Premiere Clip is another full feature video editor with an option to auto generate a video like Quik or manually edit your videos. One of the best aspects of Adobe Clip is the large selection of filters to choose from.

Check out these tips to make your mobile videos more fun to watch:

• **Combine GoPro clips with other videos** taken on your phone. Any videos or photos in your Camera Roll can be used in the video.

• **Add titles.** Give your videos some character with titles or subtitles.

• Choose the **music for the mood**. If you don't like the selections available, you can also add your own music, but remember to be aware of not using copyrighted music without permission.

• With mobile videos, **longer is not always better**. You can often make the point in a short 60 second clip, which is the maximum length of an Instagram video.

PULLING FRAME GRABS

A frame grab is a **still image (photo) taken from a video clip**. With the high video image quality on the HERO7 Silver, a still image taken from 4k video is about the same quality as an image taken in photo mode, so you can really utilize your video clips to extract amazing still images. Frame grabs pulled from videos recorded at lower resolution (1440p) will not produce the same quality as a "photo", however the quality is suitable for Instagram and many other online uses. Frame grabs pulled from video have the same resolution as the video file, so a higher resolution video produces a larger still image. Here are a couple of easy ways to pull a frame grab:

In Quik for Desktop

With the video paused on the desired frame, click the Grab a Photo icon at the bottom of the screen. Quik for Desktop will add a new thumbnail with the extracted frame.

In the GoPro App

Play the video from your camera or downloaded media using the GoPro App. Tap the Image icon at the bottom of the screen. Then scroll to the frame you want to grab and click the check mark.

In GoPro Studio

1. In Step 2 in GoPro Studio, make any aesthetic adjustments to the video before exporting your frame grab.
2. When ready to export the frame grab, slide the time bar to scroll to the exact frame you want to export. You can move forward or backwards frame by frame by using the buttons on either side of the play button.
3. In the top menu, click Share>Export Still
4. Name the file and if you want to export the file at full size, choose Native under the Size to Export dropdown menu. GoPro Studio will export a JPEG photo file to the location you chose on your computer.

After exporting a frame grab, you can adjust its appearance in a photo-editing app like you will learn about next.

PHOTO EDITING

When it comes to photography, there are lots of things you can do with a GoPro! There are tons of ways to edit photos and you will eventually find your own style. This section will help you **give your photos or frame grabs the extra pizazz** they need after coming straight from the camera.

Back in the days before digital, we selected our film based on its color and grain qualities. In the digital age, we give our photos a little more in postproduction. Even though photos straight out of the camera are presentable, raw images can always use a little help looking better. This section is written to help you process photos to make them look their best.

There are also quite a few things that are lacking when compared to a traditional camera such as a DSLR. Editing is where you can take your GoPro photos and make them stand apart. With a few simple edits, you can boost the colors, improve your photos and even mimic quite a few of the looks you would capture using a DSLR or mirrorless camera.

MOBILE PHOTO APPS

Mobile photo-editing apps offer most of the functionality of desktop-editing apps on your full resolution photos. There are tons of apps available and you can easily do all of your photo editing on mostly free apps if you choose to. For these tutorials, **editing techniques are shown using Lightroom Mobile and Snapseed**.

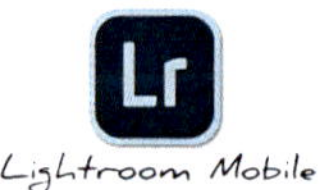

Lightroom Mobile is one of the most popular apps for professional photographers, and once you learn the techniques on your device, you can easily replicate these adjustments on your desktop if you choose to. Since some of the features require a Creative Cloud membership (which costs $10/month), Snapseed is used as an alternate for those adjustments. Pixlr is another full-featured free app to look into that has a few features not available in Lightroom or Snapseed, although the free version is full of ads.

You may already have your favorite apps, so feel free to use the following editing tips to make similar adjustments. The recommended apps may not be the best since new apps are constantly being developed. However, at the time of publication, they are some of the best and are able to make the adjustments shown in these tutorials.

There are two downsides to editing photos on a device- 1) transferring large files (it can use a lot of data and take up storage), and 2) monitoring image quality on a smaller screen. However, the convenience and ease of editing photos on your device is enticing.

If you are editing photos on a device, there are a couple of ways to access them:

1. If your files are still on your microSD card, you can use the GoPro App to wirelessly download them to your device or access the files on the Quik Key (a microSD card reader that can be inserted into your phone or tablet).

2. If you have already downloaded the footage off of the microSD card onto a computer, you can email them to yourself from your computer and save them to your device's photo library.

3. If you are a GoPro Plus subscriber, you can access your content on any device through the cloud.

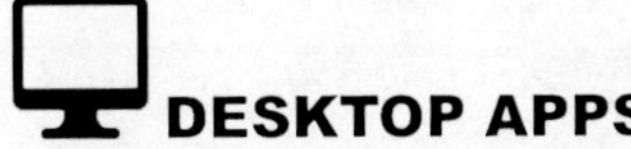

DESKTOP APPS

If you want to edit photos on your computer, Lightroom has all of the tools necessary to edit your photos like a pro- in fact, most pros use Lightroom. If you took RAW .gpr photos, RAW files can be edited in Lightroom or Camera Raw. Photoshop is only needed for more complicated editing when multiple layers are needed.

If you don't have Photoshop or Lightroom, you can get full access to both for $10 a month, which also includes the full version of Lightroom Mobile and Photoshop Fix for your device. You can also get a fully functional free 30-day trial to see if you like their apps. The author of this book is not affiliated with Adobe- it's just the industry standard. Professional editing software will make your work a lot easier and give you better results.

If you would prefer to use a free desktop program, you can use Gimp, which is free. Gimp allows you to make most of these adjustments, but Gimp usually requires a few extra steps to achieve similar results.

Whether you choose to edit photos using your device or a computer often depends on the number of photos you are editing and your final use for them, so let's move on and learn how to work some magic on your GoPro photos.

This is just one recommended workflow for adjusting your photos- there are many ways you could go about doing this. For the most efficient photo editing workflow, follow these steps in order.

Note: If you already have your own editing workflow, you can move ahead to the section on Removing Fisheye.

BASIC EDITING

Let's start with the basic editing that should be done for any photo. These little adjustments make a big impact. Although we are using Lightroom Mobile for this tutorial, similar adjustments can be made on most photo-editing programs, both desktop and mobile.

Import your photos

After you have transferred photos onto your phone, or have inserted the Quik Key, open Lightroom Mobile and select a photo to work with.

Applying Presets/Filters

Under the Presets option, scroll through the presets to see how they affect the appearance of your photos. This is like adding filters in other mobile editing apps. With experience, you will know your favorite go-to's. Or you may decide that you prefer to manually adjust the appearance of your photos.

Priime is another free mobile app with some amazing filters for your photos.

If you are using Lightroom or Photoshop on your computer, you may also want to add the Nik Collection, which is a collection of free plugins from Google. The Nik Collection contains, among other tools, a comprehensive set of filters for color correction. After you install it, access the color filters by clicking Photo>Edit In>Color Efex Pro.

Color Correction

Straight out of your camera, your photos may look a bit dull. It's easy to correct the appearance of your photos in a few simple steps to add more color and life. These adjustments are made using the Light and Color tools in Lightroom Mobile, but every decent photo-editing app has similar features. In Snapseed, they are found in Develop for RAW files or Tune for JPEGs

1. Use the Light tool to adjust Exposure, Contrast, Whites and Blacks. Exposure and Contrast are typically the most impactful adjustments to fine tune the tone of your photo.

2. Using the Color tool, the Vibrance and Saturation adjustments will add more impact to your images. When adjusting Vibrance and Saturation, add color until it looks oversaturated and then back it down a bit so the image doesn't look over edited. You will rarely go beyond +25 for Saturation, depending on the photo. If you took the photo using a manual White Balance setting, you may need to adjust White Balance or Temperature. If you used Auto White Balance, these most likely won't need to be adjusted.

3. Lastly, after other adjustments are made, use the Clarity slider in the Effects tool if the image needs more contrast and punch. The Clarity slider boosts the midtones of a photo.

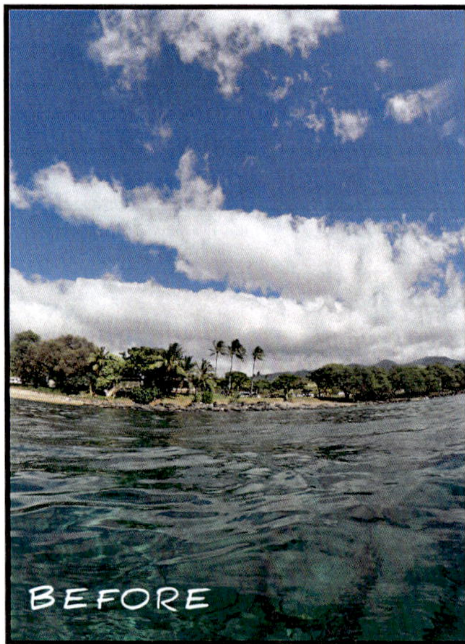

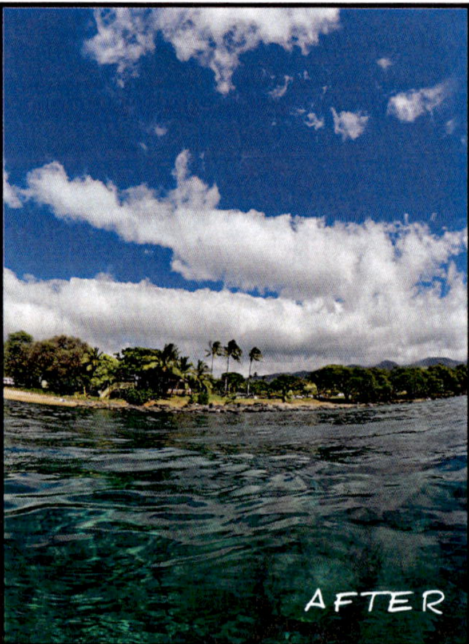

The Original photo is on the left. The image on the right was adjusted using the basic editing adjustments shown above. Here are the adjustments made: Exposure -.17, Contrast +47, Highlights -34, Whites -22, Blacks -11, Vibrance +25, Saturation +7.

These same adjustments can also be made using the Develop Module in Lightroom.

REMOVING FISHEYE

You learned how to remove the fisheye effect for video, but there is also an easy way to correct lens distortion in your photos if they need a more linear perspective.

Using the lens correction adjustment will cause some loss of the content around the edges of your photos, so make sure you don't lose anything you feel is important to the composition. Also, keep an eye on objects around the edge of the photo to make sure they don't become too stretched out in appearance.

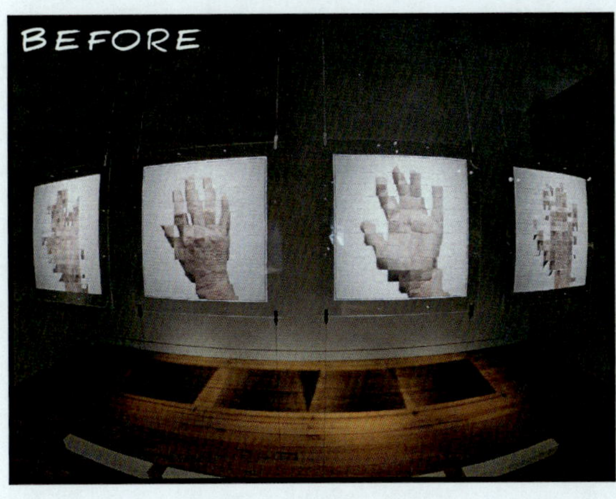

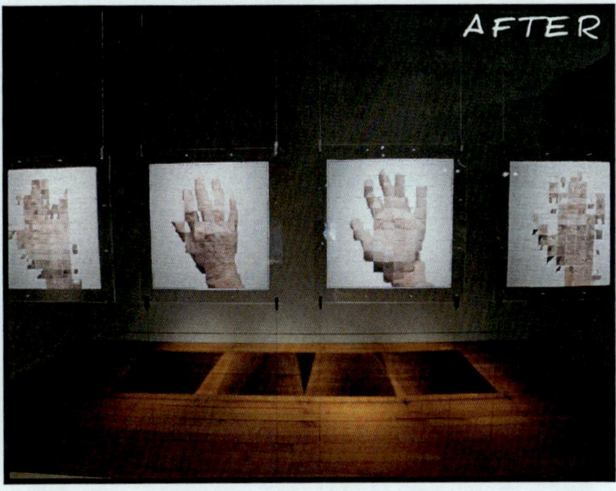

Lens corrections were made to the image on the right to remove the fisheye effect.

Since Lightroom Mobile typically takes a while for the lens profile to be added, here's how to remove the fisheye using SKRWT, which is a paid app (about $1.99US), but it's one of the best available:

1. Import your photo into SKRWT and select the curved edges icon on the bottom right.

2. Select the GoPro tab on the right. Slide the bottom bar to the positive numbers until you are happy with the results. Between 10-15 is typically a good range to remove the fisheye effect.

3. Save your image to your phone and make any additional edits using Lightroom Mobile or Snapseed.

Lightroom Mobile also has a lens profile tool to correct fisheye, but fisheye removal will not work until the HERO7 lens profiles are added. After a new camera is released, there is a delay before the lens profile is added to the app.

If you make the Lens Correction adjustment using Lightroom on your computer, you can also fine tune the amount of distortion removed using the Distortion slider. You can also make this correction in Photoshop using Filter>Lens Correction and selecting your camera model. Make sure Geometric Distortion is checked.

CROPPING

Cropping is best done after you have decided whether you want to use the lens correction option or not since the lens correction will change your photo's content.

> **TIP:** Cropping your photo is another technique you can use to remove the wide angle look of your photo. By cropping the edges of the frame and keeping the center of the image, you can remove the areas with the most distortion.

The 10 MP photos from the HERO7 Silver and White cameras give you plenty of room to crop your image and still have a high-resolution photo. Cropping is a great way to affect the composition of your photo. This is where you can get closer and get creative. If you are using the photo for Instagram or other mobile media, you don't need much resolution so feel free to be bold. Follow these steps to crop your photo in Lightroom Mobile:

1. Select the Crop Icon on the bottom toolbar at the right side of Lightroom Mobile.

2. Select your desired Aspect (square, original, etc. or you can enter custom dimensions). There are many aspect ratios to choose from when cropping depending on how you plan to use the image. Square (1:1) is obviously a common choice for social media such as Instagram. 4:3 will maintain the same proportions as your original GoPro photo.

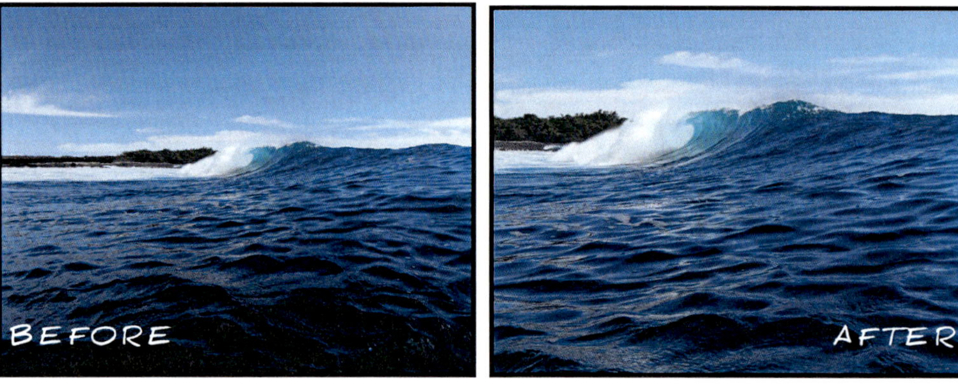

The Original image (on the left) was cropped tighter to bring the action closer to the viewer.

3. If your photo is not straight, use the Angle slider to straighten your photo.

4. Under Orientation, you can rotate or flip the photo. Change the orientation to see if another orientation creates a more enticing perspective.

5. Drag the corners of the crop box to crop your image. You can also move your image inside the box to reposition it.

6. Click the check mark to apply the cropping.

CLONING

Removing unwanted objects is much easier in a photo than in a video. Cloning is especially useful to remove sun glare. Sunspots are common when using a GoPro in backlit lighting because the wide angle lens captures so much of the sky.

You will need to turn to another app besides Lightroom Mobile for cloning, or healing, as it is often called. Most of the mobile apps, including Snapseed or Photoshop Express let you clone out unwanted areas using the Healing Brush on your touch screen.

It can be tricky to fine-tune cloning on your device, but when working in Snapseed or Photoshop Express, the more you zoom in, the patch becomes smaller and will give you better results.

If you are an Adobe Creative Cloud member, Photoshop Fix also has lots of cloning tools.

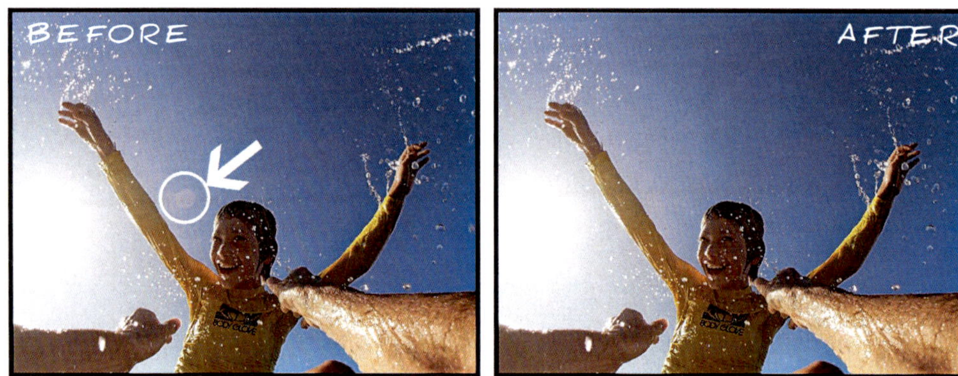

Sunspots are a common problem in photos that can be easily corrected using the Cloning/Healing Tool. The sun glare in the original photo was a minor distraction, but thanks to the Healing tool in Snapseed, it's gone in the image on the right.

SELECTIVE BLUR

When using a GoPro, everything beyond 1 foot of your camera will be in focus. This wide depth of field is great because you don't need to worry about focusing your camera.

For some photos though, you might want to mix it up by adding a shallow depth of field look as is often seen when using a DSLR. DSLR's have the option of changing aperture settings to achieve a shallow depth of field, which brings more attention to the area you want your viewers to focus on. With a shallow depth of field, only a certain distance from the camera will be in-focus. You can easily mimic this technique using a number of free apps on your device.

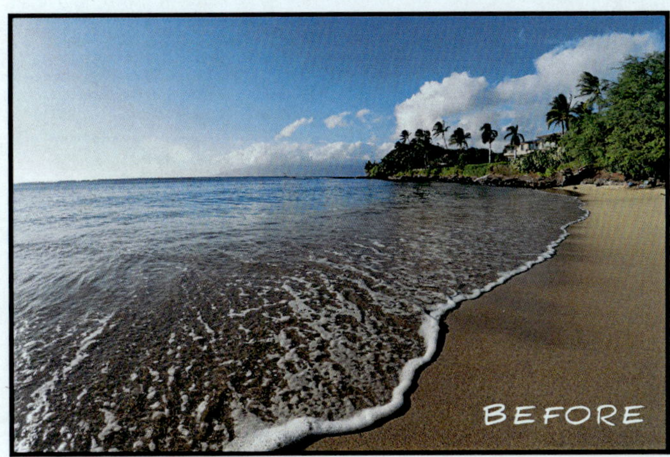

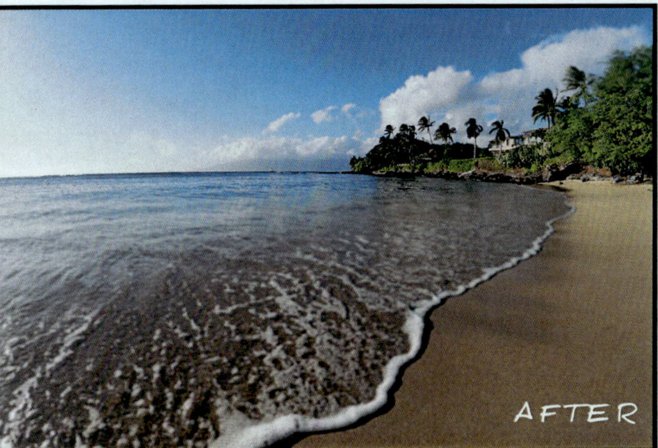

In the bottom photo, the foreground and background were blurred to create the effect of a shallow depth of field, which makes a subtle, yet very impactful difference.

You can selectively blur areas of the photo, leaving your subject in focus. This can be done for free using the Selective tool in Lightroom Mobile. Make two selective edit areas and then in the Detail tool, reduce the Sharpness to create a blurred effect. Pixlr also offers simple blur effects by using the brush and eraser tools. Photo Focus is another free app with more blur options.

Try to keep objects in focus that are along the same plane to mimic the way a DSLR would naturally capture a shallow depth of field.

FINISH IT OFF

Once you have finished editing your photos, you can finish it off by adding a few final touches.

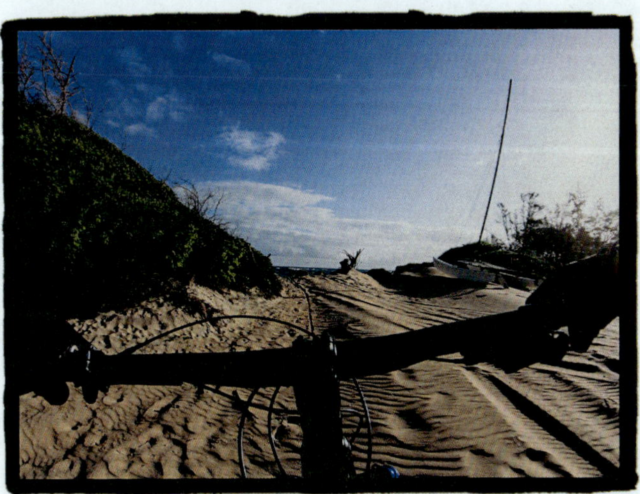

A Matte Detail filter was added using Lightroom Mobile. The Film Emulsion Edge was added in Photoshop Express. These types of filters and effects can easily be added to your photos to make them more fun!

A vignette adds a dark area around the edges of the frame, or you can choose a stylish edge, such as a film emulsion. Lightroom Mobile has vignette controls. Snapseed and Photoshop Express both have some good edge and frame options.

You can also add some fun lighting effects. Lens Distortions and Pixlr are free apps with lens flares and other effects that are easy to preview and add to your photos.

ADVANCED, BUT SUPER COOL PHOTO TIP

Make Your Photos Come To Life with the Parallax 2.5D Effect.

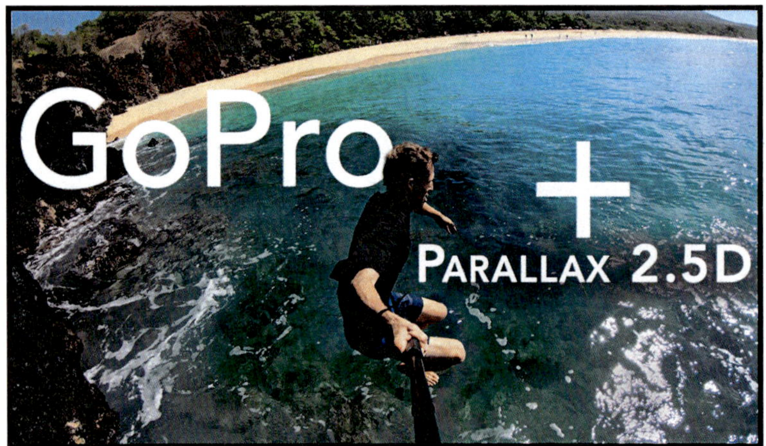

You may want to add some photos into your edited videos, but a still photo lacks movement. Adding a Ken Burns effect or using keyframes can create some movement to your photos, but if you really want the picture to come to life, check out the Parallax 2.5D effect.

Using this effect, the subject and background are edited onto separate layers. Each layer is then edited to zoom separately, creating the illusion that the subject is moving into the scene. Using Parallax 2.5D is a great way to integrate photos into your videos without them looking stale and stagnant.

If you are interested in adding a 2.5D Parallax Effect to your photos using Photoshop, you can watch a tutorial by the author of this book on YouTube at bit.ly/2lHsdzF.

RESIZING YOUR IMAGE

Your HERO7 camera produces high quality large images, but if you decide you want to print an image larger than the original file size (a 30"x40" print @ 300 DPI for example), it's best to increase the size (called upsampling) of your photo. The newest version of Photoshop does a great job of upsampling your photos.

If you are really going large (up to 1000% of the original) and want the best, there are also a few professional software options for resizing images that are even better than Photoshop. These are not free (cost is usually $100-200), but they are worth the investment if you plan to resize a bunch of images or print large wall art.

The two most popular resizing software for high quality large prints are:
Resize by OnOne Software (onOneSoftware.com)
Blow Up by Alien Skin Software (alienskin.com)

EDITING AN ACTION SEQUENCE/MULTIPLE EXPOSURE

As you learned previously, an action sequence is a digitally composited blend of photos/frames taken using Burst or Continuous photo modes with your HERO7. Video frame grabs can also be used. Tips for setting up this type of photo are provided in Step 4- Capture Your Action.

The most effective way to make an action sequence is to use a desktop photo editing program. This cool looking effect can be done using Gimp or Photoshop. This tutorial shows you how to make an action sequence using Gimp, since it is free photo-editing software. The process seems complicated at first, but once you get the hang of it, you can make these images rather quickly.

On your device, you can use SeqPic ($.99 for the version that allows you to composite multiple images) to composite your images. SeqPic lacks some editing techniques available on a desktop app, but it does a decent job on most sequences.

Steps for Editing An Action Sequence

1. Select the batch of photos you want to use for the action sequence. Open the photos in their location on your computer and drag them into a new folder with easy access. If the subject ends up overlapping too much, you can turn off some of the photo layers when you are editing.

2. Open Gimp and open the first photo of the sequence by going to File>Open and select the first photo of the sequence. Click Open.

3. Add the rest of the photos to the file you are working with by clicking File>Open As Layers. Select the rest of the photos and click Add.

4. Reverse the order of the layers so that the first photo of the sequence is on top. Go to Layer>Stack>Reverse Layer Order.

5. Next add a layer mask to the top photo (layer). A layer mask lets you select which part of the photo you want to show up. Click on the top layer in the layer bar to the right. Go to Layer>Mask>Add Layer Mask. In the dialog box that appears, select Black (Full Transparency) and click Add. The first photo of the sequence will disappear from view.

6. Now you are going to bring back the pieces of the photo that you want to show up in your action sequence. Select the Paintbrush Tool.

7. On the left side below the tools, make sure the foreground color is set to White. Painting with white will paint away the Layer Mask, bringing back your subject. (If White is set as the background color, you can click the little arrow to switch White to foreground.)

8. Paint over the area where your subject was to bring your subject back onto the screen. If you need to adjust how much you painted, switch your foreground color to black. Black will cover back up the areas you painted white. Fine tune the layer mask until you are happy with the parts of the photo that are showing up.

9. If the subject in the layer below overlaps too much with the photo you are revealing, turn off layers until you see the layer you want to appear. Turn off layers by pressing the eye icon next to the layer on the layer bar to the right.

10. Repeat steps 5 through 9 for each photo (layer) that you want to show up, except for the bottom photo.

11. Finally, in the layers bar on the right, right click (Control + Click on Mac) and select Flatten Layers. You can now make any color adjustments like you learned in the previous section.

12. Export your file by clicking File>Export and save your file as your preferred file type.

If you prefer watching a tutorial video on how to do this, you can watch one of our video tutorials on YouTube to walk you through the steps.
For the tutorial using Gimp, go to this address: http://bit.ly/1gJ3Ztf
For the tutorial using Photoshop, go to this address: http://bit.ly/GXoQv9

Now that you've edited your photos and videos, you are ready to move on to Step 6 and show them to people!

STEP SIX

SHARE IT

Get Your Vision Out There For People To See

You've made it this far, now it's time to share your masterpiece. Even if your first video or photos are not masterpieces, friends and family will be excited to finally see you in action.

GoPro has really put priority on making it easier to create your content and share it. Read on to find out the many ways you can share your photos and videos.

SHARING THROUGH THE GOPRO APP & QUIK

The GoPro App allows you to share photos and videos directly from the App. You can share files that are currently on your camera's microSD card or files you have downloaded to your device. If you want to view files when your camera is not connected, view your files on the App and save them to My Media by **clicking the small icon on the bottom right to download them to your device**.

When saving files to your device, depending on file size, the GoPro App may automatically convert your hi-res video files to a lower resolution for compatibility with your phone.

There is only limited editing directly available within the GoPro App, but you can trim a shorter clip from a longer video. The App also lets you play your video in slow motion, add GPS stickers (such as speed, path, a map, and G-force with the *Silver Only), and grab a still image from your videos. You can then share your clip to social media (such as Facebook, Instagram, etc.) or share with your friends via text messages, email or a link from GoPro's site.

For more advanced editing options on your device, use Splice or Quik as you learned about in the previous section. You can also share to social media or directly to your friends via messages and email through Quik for Desktop, Splice and Quik.

If the files are already on your computer and you want to share them to a phone or tablet, on a Mac, right click (Ctrl+Click) and select Share to select how you want to send the file (Messages, email, etc.) On a PC, select the file in its folder and use the Share Button on the Share tab to share the file.

SENDING LARGE FILES

If you were out filming and captured some great video footage of your friend or even a stranger who was out there shredding, you might be struggling to figure out how to share your video files. Even a short video file is too big for most email accounts, so you need to find a better way to share files. Dragging the file over to a USB flash drive and loading it onto your friend's computer is one rather old-school, but effective, way of sharing files.

If you don't have the convenience of physically sharing the file, there are a few free ways to send large files. (These are the current size limits at the time of publication.)

WeTransfer is probably the best free option because it lets you share files up to 2GB as often as you like without signing up for any plans. All you need to do is to enter your email and the recipient's email address and link the file.

Hightail (formerly YouSendIt) offers a free plan that lets you send files up to 100MB, which isn't much if you are sharing 4k files, but it could be sufficient for short clips or lower resolution files. You can send much larger files with the paid plans.

Jumpshare is another sharing site with 2GB of free storage and a max file size of 250MB.

SOCIAL MEDIA

Social Media and Online Sharing Sites are great ways to share your experience with the world. Social Media has undoubtedly contributed to the explosion in popularity of GoPro cameras. Many GoPro camera users are super active in social media communities. After you edit your videos and photos, here are a few FREE ways to get them out there for people to see.

Video-Sharing Sites:

YouTube - Most popular

You can create a channel and upload your videos for private or public viewing. YouTube is by far the most popular video sharing website so far, and with Google's backing, will continue to be. With a basic account and current browser, you can upload videos smaller than 128GB and less than 15 minutes in length. You can upload as many videos as you like. Once your channel gets a following of 1000 subscribers and 4000 hours watched in the last 12 months, you can even earn some extra cash from your videos by monetizing your channel, especially if one of the videos goes viral.

Vimeo - Creative/Non-commercial Videos

With a free basic account, you can upload 500MB of video per week up to 5GB total storage. The content must be original and non-commercial. You also have the option of making your videos private with password protection, which is convenient if you want to share selected videos with a limited crew.

Dailymotion - Huge Global Audience

This video-sharing site allows you to earn revenue from your videos and offers a free membership with unlimited uploads.

DropShots – Family-focused Sharing

Check out DropShots for a more personal way to share your videos (and photos) when you want to primarily share with family and friends.

Photo-Sharing Sites:

Below are a few favorites out of the plethora of free photo-sharing websites available. Every one of the sites below has free accounts, but many of them are restrictive unless you upgrade your account. Check out these sites and see which one best serves your photo sharing needs.

Flickr, 500px, Webshots, Photobucket, and ***Fotolog*** are some of the most popular photo sharing sites.

Social Media:

And of course, there are the Social Media sites we use to share our lives. Most of them allow us to upload photos and videos, or links to videos.

Facebook - Post photos & videos (either through links or natively).

Instagram - Easily share photos and short videos (currently up to 60 seconds) with a variety of fun filters and basic editing tools, as well as share links to your videos.

Pinterest - Pinterest is the perfect place to share ideas and pick up new tips on using your GoPro camera

Path - A more personal way to post photos & videos

Twitter - Post photos & links to videos

MySpace - Post photos & videos (Yes, it still exists!)

Google+ - Share photos & videos

PHOTO PRINTING

The HERO7 takes high-resolution photos that allow for a wide variety of printing options. If you use the resizing software recommended in Step 5, you can use your GoPro® camera to make almost any size print you want.

With the plethora of creative photo printing options available, here are a few of the best:

Acrylic Face Mounts

The printed photograph is mounted behind a thin layer of acrylic and usually comes with a hanger mounted to the back, so it is ready to hang. Acrylic Face Mounting creates a modern look for wall art.

It's a tricky process, but Bumblejax, Costco, and BayPhoto are a few labs that can produce these eye-popping prints for you.

Metal Prints

This printing process actually prints your photo directly onto aluminum, creating a unique modern display, with lots of shine and realism.

Google "Metal Prints" or check out BayPhoto, Costco or Bumblejax.

Wood Prints

Photos printed on wood have a very organic feel and create an instant art piece. If you print without a white under layer, the wood grain shows through your image, giving it a unique texture that is perfect for adding a personal touch to your photography.

Check out Woodsnap.com or BayPhoto, or Google "Wood Photo Prints" to find a printer who can print your photos on wood.

Gallery Wraps/Giclees

Make your photo look like a traditional wrapped piece of art by printing it on a gallery wrap. Choose Metallic Photo Paper for extra vibrancy in your photo.

Google "Gallery Wraps" or check out BayPhoto and Costco for printing options.

GATHERINGS

Use your footage as a reason to gather friends together and have a party. You are the filmmaker so have a pseudo premiere. But don't be greedy. Set your friends up to film them (if they don't have their own cameras). Edit your footage together into a mini flick and let everyone hoot and holler over the results. Here are a few ways to display your videos and photos.

Big Screen TV

Showing your videos on the Big Screen is an impressive way to watch your creation up close and personal. 4k Monitors, HD DVD Players and BluRay Players are currently the highest quality.

Digital Projector

Pop up a white movie screen and watch your footage outdoors for a truly impressive display. Digital Projectors vary in quality (usually from 720p up to 4k) and price, of course.

Computer

Computer monitors are not the most social way to show your videos, but they are usually high quality and most of them display 1080p. Some monitors display 2.7k and even 5k.

Congratulations, you now have the knowledge and power to create and share your experiences with the world! In Step 7, you will learn more tricks to take your GoPro footage to the next level.

STEP SEVEN

BEYOND THE BASICS

Take It Further

Once you have mastered the basics of using your HERO7 camera and see how much fun these cameras can be, you will probably want to add more flair and style to your videos and photos. When you are ready to add some extra features to your camera setup, these additional tips and accessories will help you get even better shots.

The list of accessories and extras that are available for your GoPro goes on and on, but in this step, we will break it down to the accessories that will make the biggest impact on your footage and on your filming experience.

4K (*Silver Only)

As you have learned, the HERO7 Silver records video footage in 4k resolution. While 4k gives you clear video and lots of freedom when it comes to editing, the high resolution is still being integrated into some of our technology.

4k is also known as Ultra High Definition (UHD) or 2160p (since other resolutions are defined by the line height and 4k refers to the width). **4k is 4x the resolution of 1080p**, which means there are 4x as many pixels in the footage. What this means for anyone watching 4k footage on a 4k monitor is incredibly clear, realistic-looking video that looks like you can jump right in. The difference can really be seen the closer you get to the screen. As you work with the hi-res videos, you will notice the difference.

If you want to watch your HERO7 Silver footage in 4k, it's best to record your footage in 4k. The HERO7 Silver records 4k at 30 frames per second with stabilization, which makes it possible to film almost everything you need in 4k.

Because of the high resolution, 4k is incredibly demanding in terms of computer performance. If you are playing back your footage through your computer connected to a 4k monitor, your computer must also be 4k compatible or the footage will most likely play back choppy. Editing long clips also requires a lot of memory. If you are having trouble editing 4k, you probably need to upgrade your computer to make it compatible for 4k playback. A flash hard drive (aka SSD), sufficient RAM and a good graphics card will greatly improve your computer's performance when editing in 4k.

If you want to watch your 4k content from your camera directly to your TV, some TV's are capable of 4k playback with a USB card reader or USB drive. Check with your TV manufacturer to check compatibility.

MORE GOPRO FEATURES

With the Hero7 Silver and White, GoPro really simplified the settings options for an easy user experience. This book attempts to cover everything these cameras CAN do, however, with the simplified settings, there are a lot of things they can't do. As your cinematography and photography knowledge expands, you will learn about more techniques and may wonder what is possible with your camera. You may also hear about other setting options and wonder why you don't know about them. The following list of features available on other GoPro cameras is included to inform and educate you about everything GoPro.

SETTINGS

ProTune- This allows fine-tuned control of advanced video and photo settings such as ISO, Shutter Speed, White Balance, Color and more. Manually adjusting these settings can reduce noise in video and affect exposure.

HyperSmooth Stabilization- This is the highest level of electronic stabilization available on GoPro cameras which is available on the Hero7 Black.

FOV (Field of View)- The Hero7 Silver and White offer only Wide Field of View, but many GoPro cameras also offer other options. Depending on the video resolution, newer models also offer a super wide field of view called SuperView and a field of view with a reduced Fisheye effect called Linear. Older models offered Medium and Narrow fields of view instead of using Touch Zoom.

SuperPhoto- Available on the Hero7 Black, SuperPhoto analyzes a scene and applies one of a few different options to enhance photos.

RAW- All of the Black cameras have the option to take photos saved as a RAW file. A RAW file saves all of the original data in an uncompressed file for more editing flexibility.

MODES

Looping Video- This video mode records for a specified length of time and then begins to loop over itself, which is useful when using a GoPro as a dashcam.

TimeWarp Video- Available only on the Hero7 Black, this mode records stabilized time lapse videos and hyperlapses.

Time Lapse Photo Mode- Instead of automatically creating a time lapse video, this mode takes photos at a set interval, which can then be used individually as a photo file or edited into a time lapse video.

Night Photo- This mode allows for an open shutter time up to 30 seconds, which is necessary to take photos at night when there is limited light.

Night Lapse Video- Night Lapse Video mode records a series of night photos for creating time lapses at night or in low light scenes.

ACCESSORIES

Removeable Battery- Many models offer a removeable battery, which allows for an easy, quick swap when the battery dies. For long filming projects, extra batteries are essential to make it through the day.

Removeable Lens Port- The lens port on the Black cameras can be removed and replaced if damaged. The design of this lens port is different than the 7 Silver/White and can accommodate a variety of filters, such as a Polarizer or ND Filter.

SuperSuit- The SuperSuit is a waterproof case made by GoPro that provides extra underwater protection to go as deep as 197' for scuba diving. The SuperSuit requires the lens port to be removed so it's not compatible with the Hero7 Silver/White. Many dome ports (aka over-under housings, 50/50 ports) require mounting the camera in the SuperSuit and are also not compatible.

LiveStream- So far, the Hero7 Black is the only GoPro camera with the capability to stream live through the GoPro App.

Stereo Audio- Some models use 3 microphones to record stereo audio and offer manual control over the recording style.

Microphone Adapter- The Hero7 Silver/White is not compatible with GoPro's mic adapter for connecting an external mic.

HDMI Port- Some models offer an HDMI port for connecting to an external monitor or TV.

Karma Drone/Grip- Many of the other models are compatible with GoPro's Karma drone and Stabilizer, but the Hero7 Silver/White is not compatible with these devices.

These accessories will instantly improve the quality of your videos and photos:

PORTABLE LIGHTING

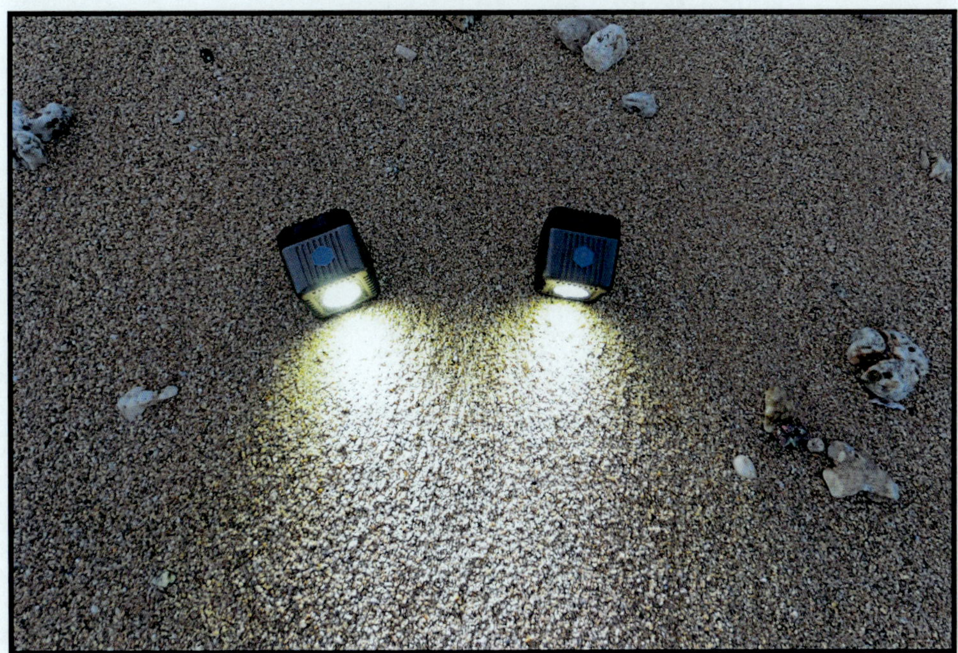

LumeCubes are waterproof and portable- excellent tools for adding light to dark scenes.

Most of your daytime lighting will come from the sun, but using an external light can extend your filming time or even just fill in light when the sunlight is not bright enough.

There are a variety of external lights that can be mounted directly to your GoPro or placed in a scene for spot lighting. LumeCubes are small cube-shaped portable lights and are one of the best options because they are waterproof to 100 feet. Just one LumeCube can put out up to 1500 lumens (that's bright). A strong (1500-2500 lumens) flashlight can also be used to add light to your scene.

For Night Video

Mount a light to your GoPro for night filming. Many of the portable light manufacturers (such as LumeCube) make a mount that allows you to mount your GoPro camera alongside their light. Night video filmed without artificial lighting requires using a high ISO setting resulting in lots of "noise". The use of a light allows your camera to bring your ISO back down a few stops, improves the view of the scene and enables you to continue GoPro'ing into the night.

As a Fill Light

In low light settings, such as under a canopy of trees or on a cloudy day, external lights can be used to fill in shadowed areas. Place the light up against a subject or one of the key landscape areas for highlighting. Or place the light behind a translucent object for backlighting.

Underwater

Light disappears quickly as its filtered through water. As you dive down under water, an external light fills back in the light, restoring color to a dull underwater scene. And if you are diving deep where it gets even darker, your own light source will be the only source of any real usable light.

PROTECT YOUR CAMERA

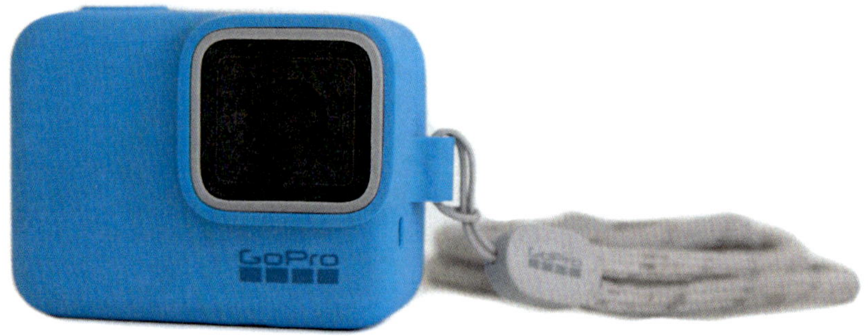

The Hero7 Silver with the GoPro Sleeve and Lanyard

GoPro cameras are made to be tough. They can handle dirt, water, mud and almost everything you can throw at it during your life's journeys. They've also been known to handle some hard knocks and heavy drops, but of course, nothing is guaranteed. The lens port on the front of the camera is not replaceable like in the Hero7 Black, so that's one part of the camera you want to pay special attention to.

Even though the Hero7 Silver or White is not a huge financial investment, there are a couple of ways to protect your camera so you don't have worry about breaking it. If you sign up for GoPro Plus, which is about $5 dollars per month, GoPro will replace your camera up to 2x per year for a reduced replacement fee ($59 for the Silver, $39 for the White as of publication). As a GoPro Plus subscriber, you can also use their cloud service to store a large amount of your video and photo files.

Another easy way to protect your camera if you want to carry it unmounted is to put it use the GoPro Sleeve and Lanyard (pictured above). The Sleeve is made of silicone which gives your camera an extra layer of protection if it falls or gets knocked.

If you really want to be able to thrash this camera without worry, GoPro (and some other companies) make Screen Protectors. Slap one on the Touch Screen to prevent it from getting scratched and you are good to go.

GIMBAL / STABILIZER

Although it has to be cheap to make sense, the mount/accessory that will make the most impact on your videos is a gimbal, also known as a stabilizer. No other accessory will have as big of an impact as a high-quality gimbal. Mounting your GoPro to a gimbal will eliminate unsightly camera shake or rocky videos. In case you don't know, a gimbal keeps the horizon straight and absorbs shock from your movements keeping the video footage smooth even when your filming technique isn't. The result is Hollywood style videos for a fraction of the cost (and much simpler for a one-person film crew like you may be).

Even if you correct your videos using post-processing stabilization techniques, they still won't match the quality you would capture using a high-quality gimbal. And even though the GoPro Hero7 Silver and White cameras have integrated electronic video stabilization (EIS), the result is still not as buttery smooth as a good gimbal.

There are basically two types of gimbals- a handheld gimbal or a mountable/wearable gimbal. Some double as both.

The Hero7 Silver and White cameras are not compatible with the GoPro Karma Grip made by GoPro (the Karma Grip's price tag doesn't make sense for the Hero7 Silver or White cameras anyways). It's cheaper to upgrade to the Hero7 Black, which has built-in gimbal-like stabilization.

However, because a gimbal stabilizes your footage and keeps a straight horizon (something the Hero7 Black doesn't do), it may be worthwhile to purchase a cheap gimbal, such as the Hohem iSteady Pro.

The downsides of a gimbal

• Most gimbals are not waterproof, so this limits their use in certain water activities or extreme weather conditions.

• Gimbals are sensitive electronic devices- meaning they can break! They are pretty tough, but not tough enough for many of the activities a GoPro is used for filming.

• Audio can be a problem. Some gimbals have a tendency to block one or more of the GoPro's microphones. Others emit a small electronic noise that can be heard on your videos. It really depends on how important your audio is.

Tips for using a gimbal

• A gimbal will compensate for a lot of your erratic movements, but if you try to film using stable filming techniques (using some filming techniques from Step 4) along with a gimbal, your footage will be amazingly smooth.

• Don't subject your gimbal to sudden changes in wind- for example, sticking it out of the window in a moving vehicle. It is a sensitive electronic device that can be damaged rather easily.

OFF THE GRID HERO7 SETUP

GoPro camera enthusiasts live outside of the box. With these accessories, you can step away from a wall socket and your computer for days or weeks and still be able to record your adventures:

Portable Battery Charger

Out of the box, the only way to charge your HERO7 is to plug it into your computer or wall charger and wait for the batteries to refill. The GoPro Auto Charger or Wall Charger lets you recharge with a wall socket or your vehicle's lighter socket giving you the freedom to get out there and disconnect. A portable power bank, like GoPro's Portable Power Pack, also comes in handy for a few charges when you are totally out there. You can also use any portable USB charger or USB phone charger as long as it outputs 5V and 1-2 Amps. Since the Hero7 Silver/White battery is built in and cannot be swapped out for a fresh one, a portable USB charger gives you the ability to recharge your camera in between sessions or during downtime.

For real freedom from the grid for long trips through rural areas, a portable USB solar charger may be your ticket to ride.

Portable Data Storage

If you know you are going to be capturing lots of footage without being able to offload onto a computer, the best option is to bring a few high capacity (128 or 256GB) microSD cards. When you fill one up, swap it out for a new one and keep it in a safe spot. Another option is to use a portable memory card backup device to store your photos and videos if you don't want to travel light. The Gnarbox Portable Backup & Editing System pretty much eliminates the need to travel with a laptop, giving you storage and editing capabilities in one portable device for the content creator who really wants to roam free. This will give you plenty of storage to empty your memory card, get some editing done in your down time and keep filming as you wander on.

TIP: Thanks for reading! If you purchased this print book new through your account, you can pick up a free digital copy of this book through the sales page where you bought it. It's part of the Matchbook program and offered for free by the author so you can also keep a copy of this book on your device.

Now get out there and have fun!

TROUBLESHOOTING

These are some of the most common problems GoPro users have run into with previous camera models. If you encounter any of these problems, try these solutions first. You can always contact GoPro's customer support via telephone and they will troubleshoot any problems with you right away. See GoPro's website for their customer service contact info for your country.

CAMERA MALFUNCTIONS

If you experience any of the following problems: **first try the solution offered**. If the problem happens repeatedly, **reinstall your camera's firmware** by performing an update through GoPro's website, through the GoPro App or through Quik for Desktop. It's possible that the firmware did not install properly during the initial installation. If the problem persists, contact GoPro's customer support.

Problem: The camera heats up when recording.
Solution: This is normal, especially when filming at 4k or 60 FPS. If you continue to experience overheating, turn off the WiFi or temporarily turn off your camera to let it cool down. Also, recording in short stints will reduce the strain on your camera.

Problem: The camera freezes up and stops responding.
Solution: This is not normal and could indicate a problem with the installation of the firmware or communication with the microSD card. Make sure to use a compatible microSD card with a large storage capacity to prevent using a maxed-out card. Unfortunately if your camera is unresponsive, since there is no way of manually shutting down the power, you will need to wait until the battery runs out, recharge your camera and start fresh. If it continues to happen, try manually reinstalling the firmware through the Support page on GoPro's website.

Problem: The camera stops recording or only records short clips.
Solution: First, check to make sure the Clip feature is not turned on. If the video repeatedly stops recording, offload your video footage to your phone or computer. After your footage is backed up, format the memory card under Preferences>Reset>Format SD Card. **This will erase all of the files on the card.** If the problem persists, another option is to reset your camera in Preferences>Reset>Factory Reset.

PLAYBACK ISSUES

Problem: Your computer does not recognize the memory card when your camera is connected to your computer.
Solution: Make sure your computer is running the current operating system.

For Mac Users: Some programs may interfere with the communication between your camera and computer. Quik for Desktop should recognize your camera, but if not, you can also import the footage using Image Capture, which is located in your Applications.

Alternatively, if your computer has an SD Card slot, remove the microSD card and use the microSD card adapter to transfer your files.

Problem: There is only audio and no picture.
Solution: Reinstall your camera's firmware by performing an update through GoPro's website, through the GoPro App or through Quik for Desktop. If the problem continues, contact GoPro's customer support. You may need to get a replacement camera.

Problem: Choppy video playback. Some users experience choppy video playback. This is mainly due to the highly-compressed video files that require a lot of work from your computer. The HERO7 uses a compression codec called H.264 to store a lot of video footage in a relatively small amount of memory. Your computer will most likely have the most trouble playing 4k files. The good news is that your files are recorded properly. The not-so-good news is that your computer may not be able to handle the large video files.

Solution: First make sure you transfer your files to a folder on your computer before attempting to view them.

Next, import your video into GoPro Studio and convert the portions of the clips you want to watch. In Step 2: Edit of GoPro Studio, if your video is still playing choppy, set the playback quality to Better (Half Resolution) or even Good (Quarter Resolution) if you are still experiencing choppy playback. This will allow most computers to play the video footage smoothly, as it should be seen.

If you are still experiencing choppy playback, check to make sure your computer meets the minimum system requirements as shown in the User Manual. If your computer does not meet these requirements, you may need to update your computer.

RECOMMENDED MICROSD CARDS

The following chart shows the microSD cards that have been tested and approved by GoPro for use with the Hero7 Silver and White cameras. Using a recommended microSD Card will reduce the chance of freezing and recording errors.

Card Name	Model #	HERO7 Black	HERO7 Silver	HERO7 White
SanDisk Extreme UHS-I 32GB	SDSDQXL-032G-A46A or SDSQXNE-032G-AN6MA	Y	Y	Y
SanDisk Extreme UHS-I 64GB	SDSDQXL-064G-A46A or SDSQXNE-064G-AN6MA	Y	Y	Y
SanDisk Pixtor Advanced 32GB	SDSDQX-032G-AB46A or SDSQXSG-032G-ABCCA	Y	Y	Y
SanDisk Pixtor Advanced 64GB	SDSDQX-064G-AB46A or SDSQXSG-064G-ABCCA	Y	Y	Y
SanDisk Extreme (UHS 3 / V30) A1	SDSQXAF-032G-GN6MA	Y	Y	Y
SanDisk Extreme PLUS UHS-I 32GB	SDSQXWG-032G-ANCMA	Y	Y	Y
SanDisk Extreme PLUS UHS-I 64GB	SDSQXWG-064G-ANCMA	Y	Y	Y
SanDisk ExtremePro (UHS 3 / V30) A1	SDSQXCG-032G-GN6MA	Y	Y	Y
SanDisk Extreme PLUS microSDHC UHS-I (UHS3 / V30 / A1)	SDSQXBG-032G-GN6MA	Y	Y	Y
SanDisk Extreme PRO microSDXC UHS-II (UHS3 / V30)	SDSQXPJ-064G-ANCM3	Y	Y	Y
Lexar 1000x microSDXC UHS-3 128GB	LSDMI128CBNL1000R	Y	Y	Y
Samsung Pro UHS-I 16GB	MB-MG16DA/AM	Y	Y	Y
Samsung Pro Endurance UHS-I 32GB	MB-MJ32GA/AM	N	Y	Y
Samsung Pro Endurance UHS-I 64GB	MB-MJ64GA/AM	N	Y	Y
Samsung Pro Endurance UHS-I 128GB	MB-MJ128GA/AM	N	Y	Y
Samsung EVO Select 128GB	MB-ME128GA/AM	Y	Y	Y
Samsung EVO Select 256GB	MB-ME256GA/AM	Y	Y	Y
Samsung EVO Plus 128GB	MB-MC128GA/AM	Y	Y	Y
Samsung EVO Plus 256GB	MB-MC256GA/AM	Y	Y	Y
Sony SR-UZA series 64GB	SR-64UZA/T	Y	Y	Y
Sony SR-UZA series 128GB	SR-128UZA/T	Y	Y	Y

If you are experiencing any other issues with your HERO7 or any of GoPro's other products, contact their Support team.

Made in United States
North Haven, CT
05 December 2024

61759213R00062